Memorizing God's Word:™ HIStory
(NIV)

Seeing Jesus in Genesis Chapter One

R. M. Lewis

WestBow
PRESS
A DIVISION OF THOMAS NELSON

WestBow Press books may be ordered through booksellers or by contacting:

WestBow Press
A Division of Thomas Nelson
1663 Liberty Drive
Bloomington, IN 47403
www.westbowpress.com
1-(866) 928-1240

Because of the dynamic nature of the Internet, any web addresses or links contained in this book may have changed since publication and may no longer be valid. The views expressed in this work are solely those of the author and do not necessarily reflect the views of the publisher, and the publisher hereby disclaims any responsibility for them.

ISBN: 978-1-4497-1487-1 (sc)

Library of Congress Cataloguing-in-Publication Data 2011925409

Scripture quotations are taken from THE HOLY BIBLE, NEW INTERNATIONAL VERSION ®, NIV ® Copyright © 1973, 1978, 1984 by Biblica, Inc.™
Used by permission of Zondervan. All rights reserved worldwide.
WWW. ZONDERVAN.COM

Cover concept and illustration by R. M. Lewis. All rights reserved.

The FLOW Coding Method is a trademark registered in the United States Patent and Trademark Offices by R. M. Lewis. savingfaith2011@gmail.com

Printed in the United States of America

WestBow Press rev. date: 3/23/2011

*This book is dedicated to all the pastors
and Bible teachers in my life from infancy.*

*It also is dedicated to publishers who
meticulously preserve the sacred trust of
word for word translations of the Holy Bible
from reliable copies of ancient manuscripts.
Without word for word translations, I could
not have written this book.*

*A special thank you to Joyce Strickland
and Janet Norman for editorial services.*

*I thank my family and my prayer partner –
best friends who enrich my life with prayer,
support, and joy.*

*To my prayer partner – best friends, what
a joyous time being with you at my 40th
wedding anniversary! Some of you were
present for the 25th celebration, but this
time was exceptional with the effort of
country-wide travel and your wonderful
testimonies enjoyed by so many loved ones.*

*Above all my love, devotion, and adulation
to my Savior and Lord Jesus Christ for
without abiding in You, I am nothing.*

CONTENTS
New International Version

I.   Seeing Jesus in Creation   9
     A.   The Quest   9
     B.   Creator God   11

II. Demonstrating the FLOW Coding Method ®   13

III. Memorizing Tips   15

IV. Mastering Long Passages   17

V.   Practicing What You Have Learned   19

VI. Resource of FLOW Coded™ Scriptures: Overviews   23
     A.   FLOW   23
     B.   Analogy   25

VII. Resource of Scriptures: Seeing Jesus in Creation   27
     A.   Day 1: Knowing Him / Foundation   27
     B.   Day 2: Saving Faith / Salvation   39
     C.   Day 3: Standing Secure / Assurance   59
     D.   Day 4: Becoming Christlike / Transformation   71
     E.   Day 5: Glorifying God / Maturation   85
     F.   Day 6: Anticipating Heaven / Kingdom   101
     G.   Day 7: Living Hope / Meditation   121

     Epilogue: The Essentials   129
          How to Be Saved / Receive Christ in Your Heart   129
          Lordship: Two Greatest Commandments   129
          The Holy Bible: The Living Word of God   129

I. SEEING JESUS IN CREATION: THE QUEST

My fascination with "Seeing Jesus in Creation" began more than twelve years ago. It began with a question of why did God bless the entirety of Creation as "good," but did not include "it was good" on the second day.

I read other reliable word for word Bible translations and "good" was definitely not there for Creation Day Two. It was also noteworthy that "the light" on Creation Day One was different from the "lights made" on Creation Day Four.

My curiosity was energized as to why? Was there an analogy related to the omission of "good" on the second day, and the distinction between the light on the first day of Creation and the lights on Day Four? Those two facts were so exciting to ponder as I read the Bible and listened to Scripture.

I made an elementary sketch of the days of Creation early one morning, because after midnight I would study the Bible and meditate. That was my time with God in silence without interruption.

Subsequent drawings were made after my first one shredded from frequent use. The date of a later sketch is January 12, 1999.

When a particular Scripture was illuminated, I would be ecstatic. Scripture references, notes, and additional details would be added to the sketch.

It seemed reasonable that if there was an analogy, it could only be about the ministry of Jesus. My mind was intrigued with the hope of seeing Jesus in Creation.

The quest was on with exuberance. My lifestyle of reading the Bible from cover to cover took on a new intensity as I searched for Jesus. The front cover of this book is designed from the old drawings from 1999.

The collection of Bible verses in this book represent more than a decade of pondering with God usually between the hours of 1:30 a.m. to 3:30 a.m. and/or 3:00 a.m. to 5:00 a.m. This was supreme private time with God, and it still thrills me.

"Seeing Jesus in Creation" is an analogy; it is not theological doctrine. It is merely my perspective of viewing Scriptures about Jesus and the church through the narrative of Genesis Chapter One.

This book has a dual purpose. My first purpose is to share some interesting insights from God's work in Creation and Jesus' work on earth. My second purpose is to demonstrate the FLOW Coding Method ® for memorizing God's Word.

My hope is that you enjoy the scriptural narrative about Jesus Christ which dovetails Bible verses from Genesis Chapter One into a synopsis of HIStory. After reading the next page, please proceed to page 25, the Analogy Overview.

Back pages are intentionally left blank except for analogy pages.

Seeing Jesus in Creation: Creator God

Is it possible to see the Lord Jesus Christ in Genesis Chapter One? Are there Bible verses about the earthly ministry of Jesus Christ that could be interwoven into Days One through Seven?

The Holy Bible from Genesis to Revelation declares HIStory, but in particular in Genesis Chapter One, there are dovetailing Bible verses for:

Day 1: Knowing Him / Foundation
Day 2: Saving Faith / Salvation
Day 3: Standing Secure / Assurance
Day 4: Becoming Christlike / Transformation
Day 5: Glorifying God / Maturation
Day 6: Anticipating Heaven / Kingdom, and
Day 7: Living Hope / Meditation.

"The Quest" on page 9 summarizes how this search began. The analogy of Genesis Chapter One, "Seeing Jesus in Creation," is in the Resource of Scriptures. It begins on page 25. The Holy Bible declares:

1. And the Word was with God, and the Word was God. He [Jesus] was with God in the beginning.   John 1:1b,2

2. He is before all things, and in him all things hold together.   Col. 1:17

3. For by him all things were created: things in heaven and on earth, visible and invisible, whether thrones or powers or rulers or authorities; all things were created by him and for him.   Col. 1:16

4. And he is the head of the body, the church ... that in everything he might have the supremacy.   Col. 1:18

5. Through him all things were made; without him nothing was made that has been made.   John 1:3

6. For God was pleased to have all his fullness dwell in him, and through him to reconcile to himself all things, whether things on earth or things in heaven, by making peace through his blood, shed on the cross.   Col. 1:19,20

7. This is how God showed his love among us: He sent his one and only Son into the world that we might live through him.   1 John 4:9

8. God made him who had no sin to be sin for us, so that in him we might become the righteousness of God.   2 Cor. 5:21

9. For there is one God and one mediator between God and men, the man Christ Jesus, who gave himself as a ransom for all men – the testimony given in its proper time.   1 Tim. 2:5,6

The tool for memorizing Scriptures of HIStory in this book, is the FLOW Coding Method ®. This system is an easy tool that immediately and successfully works. It is basically a two-part process: (1) visualizing a Bible verse in phrases, and (2) Coding or writing the first letter of each word in the phrase. "**FLOW**" is an acronym for:

*F*irst
*L*etter
*O*f
*W*ord™.

This book explains in detail how to use the FLOW Method™. Depending on the verse, an already coded Bible verse takes five minutes to memorize. Once memorized, the Holy Spirit can illuminate that Scripture in your heart at anytime. **Please proceed to page 25, the Analogy Overview.**

II. DEMONSTRATING THE FLOW CODING METHOD ®
The Nine Steps

1. Ask God to help you.
Pray for His help in understanding and in memorizing the Scripture.

2. Read aloud the verse.
Use your senses of **seeing, speaking**, and **hearing** to stimulate your memory.

Unformatted Verse Example:

John 3:17
For God did not send his Son into the world to condemn the world, but to save the world through him.

3. Visualize writing the verse in phrases using a separate line for each phrase.
Observe how to divide the verse into short, comfortable phrases.

4. Write the verse in Phrase-format with its address before and after the verse.
A verse can be formatted into phrases by concepts, natural pauses of thought, punctuation, and by placing difficult to remember words on a separate line.

```
Phrase-formatted Verse Example:

    John 3:17
    For God did not send
    his Son into the world
    to condemn the world,   but
    to save the world
    through him.
                          John 3:17
```

5. Code the Phrase-formatted verse by writing the first letter of each word.
FLOW is the acronym for Coding or writing the *First Letter Of* each *Word*.

Leave a blank line to prompt your memory for the second address or reference.

```
FLOW Coded Verse Example:
    John 3:17
    F G d n s
    h S i t w
    t c t w,  b
    t s t w
    t h.
    Address_____
```

6. Read aloud the Phrase-formatted verse with its address three or more times. PAUSE after each line.
Read with emphasis or repeat a difficult to remember phrase three times. For example, read aloud three times:

" ... to condemn the world,   but ... "

7. Use the Code to say aloud the verse with its address three or more times.
Repeat difficult lines three or more times. Look back at the words as needed. If you keep forgetting certain words, re-read aloud the Phrase-formatted verse several times before using the Code again. For example:

```
John 3:17
F G d n s      (recite with emphasis)
h S i t w      (recite with emphasis)
t c t w,  b    (repeat three times)
t s t w        (recite with emphasis)
t h.           (recite with emphasis)
Address_____
```

8. Recite aloud the verse from memory while visualizing the Code.

9. Thank God for helping you. Review often with the Code first, then the verse.

III.   MEMORIZING TIPS

1. If a verse is already Phrase-formatted™ and Coded, use a half sheet of paper to cover the Code, or glue the verse to an index card, and use the reverse side for the Code. **Read the verse out loud three times. Pause after each line**.

2. When Phrase-formatting™ a verse, use large type, and write the Scripture reference or address before and after the verse(s). Read aloud the reference/address each time.

3. When Coding a verse, leave the second address line blank to prompt your memory for the reference. Say the reference out loud.

4. When memorizing consecutive verses, write the reference number beside each verse if you like.

5. As needed, also number the lines (1, 2, 3, etc.) to prevent skipping a line as you practice.

6. When Phrase-formatting™, look for patterns in a verse, for example, repeated concepts, words, parts of speech, etc.

7. Experiment with memory prompts: spacial alignments within a line, indentation for various parts of speech, italics, color-coding, bold print, and underlining.

8. If a verse is difficult to remember, Phrase-format™ the Scripture with more memory prompts. Also in rapid succession, repeat three times or recite with emphasis any forgotten line. As you use the FLOW Coding Method ®, customize your prompts.

9. Memory prompts that can be used to enhance memorization are: shorter Phrase-formatted™ lines and spacial alignments.

10. If a Bible translation does not capitalize the pronouns referring to God, consider bold print, underlining, or color-coding **His** pronouns to increase comprehension.

11. At the end of a line if you triple space before the conjunction "and" as well as the pronoun "that", it will prompt your memory for the next word. The same could be done for other conjunctions if you so desire.

12. Possessive words could be coded with 's. For example, "those who are Christ's" is coded as "t w a C's." Keep the punctuation of hyphens and dashes. For example, "I – My" is coded as "I – M."

Isaiah 45:12a	Is. 45:12a
I have made the earth, And	I h m t e, A
created man on it.	c m o i.
I – My hands –	I – M h –
stretched out	s o
the heavens,	t h,
Is. 45:12a (NKJV)	Addr._____

13. To enhance retention, observe the first word of each Phrase-formatted™ line, and read aloud three times the sequence of first words. Please refer to the verse above and speak: **I, created, I – My, stretched, the.** Now read the Phrase-formatted™ verse.

14. When reading or reciting Bible verses, remember to: **Speak out loud at least three times, and PAUSE after each line.**

IV. MASTERING LONG PASSAGES

1. Read aloud the entire passage of Bible verses for understanding.

2. Re-read aloud the passage noting the natural flow of concepts, words, and parts of speech for Phrase-formatting™ the verses. If possible, use only one line for each verse.

3. Divide the passage into groups of verses. Memorize one group then recite from the beginning before memorizing the next group.

4. Consider using bold print, underlining, or color-coding for references to God. For example: **"to the Lord"** and **"His name."**

5. Use *italics* for verbs. This will prompt your memory that a *verb* comes next.

6. With a lengthy passage, use additional lines and spaces only as needed. Write the reference number beside each Bible verse. **Read out loud. PAUSE after each line.**

7. When a verse is difficult to remember, practice repeating three times and/or reciting with emphasis a line. For example:

Isaiah 45:18

For this is what	the LORD says –	(emphasis)
he who created the heavens,		(repeat three times)
he is God;		(emphasis)
he who fashioned	and	(emphasis)
made the earth ...		(emphasis)
I am the LORD,	and	(emphasis)
there is no other.		(repeat three times)

Is. 45:18

Isaiah 45:18

F t i w	t L s –	(with emphasis)
h w c t h,		(repeat three times)
h i G;		(with emphasis)
h w f	a	(with emphasis)
m t e ...		(with emphasis)
I a t L,	a	(with emphasis)
t i n o.		(repeat three times)

Address_____

8. Create a Memory Barcode prompt at the top of long passages. Please refer to below and "Practicing What You Have Learned."

Memory Barcode™ Phrase-formatted Example

Note: At the top of the group of verses below is a Memory Barcode; it lists verse reference numbers **6,7,** and **8,** and the first letter of each verse and its subordinate line(s). The Scripture below is formatted to have references to **God in bold print,** and *verbs* and some *adverbs* in *italics.* The letters in the Memory Barcode retain the capitalization, bold print, and italics of the first letter of each line. (Psalm 33:6-14 is on page 21.)

Psalm 33:6-8	**FLOW Coded™**
6 7 8	**6 7 8**
Bt Hh *Ll*	**Bt Hh** *Ll*
6 **By the word of the LORD** *were* the heavens *made,*	6 **B t w o t L** *w* t h *m,*
their starry host **by the breath of his mouth.**	t s h **b t b o h m.**
7 **He** *gathers* the waters of the sea into jars;	7 **H** *g* t w o t s i j;
he *puts* the deep into storehouses.	**h** *p* t d i s.
8 *Let* all the earth *fear* **the LORD;**	8 *L* a t e *f t* **L;**
let all the people of the world *revere* **him.**	*l* a t p o t w *r* **h.**

V. PRACTICING WHAT YOU HAVE LEARNED
(Be **doers** of the 9 Steps)

A. SHORT VERSE UNFORMATTED EXAMPLE:
He is the image of the invisible God, the firstborn over all creation. Colossians 1:15

Phrase-formatted™	**FLOW Coded™**
Colossians 1:15	Colossians 1:15
[Jesus] He is the image	H i t i
of the invisible God,	o t i G,
the firstborn over all creation.	t f o a c.
Col. 1:15	Addr._____

B. MORE DIFFICULT VERSE UNFORMATTED EXAMPLE:
For since the creation of the world God's invisible qualities – his eternal power and divine nature – have been clearly seen, being understood from what has been made, so that men are without excuse. Rom. 1:20

Phrase-formatted™ by Punctuation	**FLOW Coded™**
Romans 1:20	Romans 1:20
For since the creation of the world God's invisible qualities –	F s t c o t w G's i q –
his eternal power and divine nature –	h e p a d n –
have been clearly seen,	h b c s,
being understood from what has been made,	b u f w h b m,
so that men are without excuse.	s t m a w e.
Rom. 1:20	Addr._____

Phrase-formatted™ by Thought Pauses	**FLOW Coded™**
Romans 1:20	Romans 1:20
For since the creation of the world	F s t c o t w
God's invisible qualities –	G's i q –
his eternal power and divine nature –	h e p a d n –
have been clearly seen,	h b c s,
being understood from what has been made,	b u f w h b m,
so that men are without excuse.	s t m a w e.
Rom. 1:20	Addr._____

Phrase-formatted™ with Memory Prompts	**FLOW Coded™**
Romans 1:20	Romans 1:20
For since the creation of the world	F s t c o t w
God's invisible qualities –	G's i q –
his eternal power and divine nature –	h e p a d n –
have been clearly seen,	h b c s,
being understood from	b u f
what has been made, so that	w h b m, s t
men are without excuse.	m a w e.
Rom. 1:20	Addr._____

Practicing What You Have Learned
(Be **doers** of the 9 Steps)

C. LONG PASSAGE UNFORMATTED EXAMPLE:

Psalm 33:6-14

6 By the word of the LORD were the heavens made,
their starry host by the breath of his mouth.
7 He gathers the waters of the sea into jars;
he puts the deep into storehouses.
8 Let all the earth fear the LORD;
let all the people of the world revere him.
9 For he spoke, and it came to be;
he commanded, and it stood firm.
10 The LORD foils the plans of the nations;
he thwarts the purposes of the peoples.

11 But the plans of the LORD stand firm forever,
the purposes of his heart through all generations.
12 Blessed is the nation whose God is the LORD,
the people he chose for his inheritance.
13 From heaven the LORD looks down
and sees all mankind;
14 from his dwelling place
he watches all who live on earth –

Memory Barcode™ Phrase-formatted Passage
Psalm 33:6-14

6	7	8	9	10	11	12	13	14
Bt	Hh	*Ll*	Fh	Th	Bt	Bt	Fa	fh

6 **By the word of the LORD** *were* the heavens *made,*
their starry host **by the breath of his mouth.**
7 **He** *gathers* the waters of the sea into jars;
he *puts* the deep into storehouses.

8 *Let* all the earth *fear* **the LORD;**
let all the people of the world *revere* **him.**
9 For **he** *spoke,* and it *came to be;*
he *commanded,* and it *stood* firm.

10 **The LORD** *foils* the plans of the nations;
he *thwarts* the purposes of the peoples.
11 But **the plans of the LORD** *stand* firm forever,
the purposes **of his heart** through all generations.
12 Blessed *is* the nation whose **God** *is* **the LORD,**
the people **he** *chose* **for his inheritance.**

13 **From heaven the LORD** *looks down*
and *sees* all mankind;
14 **from his dwelling place**
he *watches* all who *live* on earth –
Ps. 33:6-14

FLOW Coded™
Psalm 33:6-14

6	7	8	9	10	11	12	13	14
Bt	Hh	*Ll*	Fh	Th	Bt	Bt	Fa	fh

6 **B t w o t L** *w* t h *m,*
t s h **b t b o h m.**
7 **H** *g* t w o t s i j;
h *p* t d i s.

8 *L* a t e *f* t **L;**
l a t p o t w *r* **h.**
9 F **h** *s,* a i *c t b;*
h *c,* a i *s* f.

10 **T L** *f* t p o t n;
h *t* t p o t p.
11 **B t p o t L** *s* f f,
t p **o h h** t a g.
12 B *i* t n w **G** *i* t **L,**
t p **h** *c* **f h i.**

13 **F h t L** *l d*
a *s* a m;
14 **f h d p**
h *w* a w *l* o e –
Addr._____

FLOW OVERVIEW

The Scriptures in this section are a narrative of God's work at Creation and Christ's work on earth. The Bible verses are formatted for memorization using the FLOW Coding Method ®.

In this Resource of FLOW Coded™ Scriptures, the Scriptures for each day of Creation are interwoven with corresponding Bible verses. For the pure delight of the Word of God, first read the Scriptures, then experiment with the method.

Effective helps and suggestions for using the method are included in the chapters on: Demonstrating the FLOW Coding Method ®; Memorizing Tips; Mastering Long Passages; and Practicing What You Have Learned.

If you follow the instructions in the above sections, you have the tools to implement the FLOW Method™ and to enjoy how it works. There is no exact way of using the technique. If you have a better method of coding Scripture, use it.

After reading the Resource of Scriptures section, select your own verses to be memorized. For a quick start, use a half sheet of paper to cover the Code, or fold a two-column page in this section of the book and begin practicing. You will enjoy the results.

ANALOGY OVERVIEW

Analogy: a partial likeness between two things that are compared. The following analogies view the Scriptures about Jesus and the church through Genesis Chapter One. The first page of each Analogy is the synopsis. The second page is the Genesis account for that day of Creation and the correlation. The pages following the Analogy have corresponding Bible verses interwoven with the Genesis account. I have highlighted, "God said that it was good."

Creation	God's Work at Creation	Jesus' Work on Earth	Analogy
DAY 1	The Light	Incarnation	Page 27, 28
DAY 2	Firmament / Expanse	Crucifixion	Page 39, 40
DAY 3	Earth and Vegetation	Burial and Resurrection	Page 59, 60
DAY 4	Lights	Witnesses	Page 71, 72
DAY 5	Fish and Birds	Great Commission and Pentecost	Page 85, 86
DAY 6	Adam and His Bride	Christ and His Bride	Page 101, 102
DAY 7	God Rested	Jesus Christ Rested	Page 121, 122

DAY ONE: ANALOGY SYNOPSIS

On Creation Day One,
God's work in Creation was to send a unique light.

This reminds me of God the Father sending Jesus,
the true Light to the world.

ANALOGY: CREATION DAY ONE

Analogy: a partial likeness between two things that are compared. This analogy seeks to view the Scriptures about Jesus and the church through the narrative of Genesis Chapter One.

Creation Day 1: Genesis 1:1-5

1 In the beginning God created the heavens and the earth. 2 Now the earth was formless and empty, darkness was over the surface of the deep, and the Spirit of God was hovering over the waters. 3 And God said, "Let there be light," and there was light. 4 God saw that the light was good, and He separated the light from the darkness. 5 God called the light "day," and the darkness he called "night." And there was evening, and there was morning – the first day.

God's Work in Creation: God said, "Let there be light." Light is given or sent.

Jesus' Work on Earth: Incarnation: God the Father gave Jesus, the true Light, to the world.

Bible Verse Keywords: Light; true Light; life; must work; morning star; the bright Morning Star; a light has dawned; God saw that the light was good.

Pondered: 1. The Holy Bible is replete with Scriptures proclaiming that the world was made "by", "for", "in", and "through" Jesus Christ. Please refer to "Seeing Jesus in Creation: Creator God" on page 11.

2. The lights on Creation Day Four are made. Note the distinction between the "made lights" on Creation Day Four from "the light" on Day One.
Creation Day Four:
Genesis 1:14 And God said, "Let there be lights in the expanse of the sky to separate the day from the night, and let them serve as signs to mark seasons and days and years, 15 and let them be lights in the expanse of the sky to give light on the earth." And it was so. 16 God made two great lights – the greater light to govern the day and the lesser light to govern the night. He also made the stars. 17 God set them in the expanse of the sky to give light on the earth, 18 to govern the day and the night, and to separate light from darkness. And God saw that it was good. 19 And there was evening, and there was morning – the fourth day.

Creation Day One:
3 And God said, "Let there be light," and there was light. 4 God saw that the light was good, and He separated the light from the darkness. 5 God called the light "day," and the darkness he called "night." And there was evening, and there was morning – the first day.

3. On Creation Days Three through Six, the Bible declares, "And God saw that it was good." Only on Creation Day One, does God identify "it." The Scripture heralds, "God saw that the light was good ... ."

4. Could it be that this unique "light" is an analogy of Jesus, the "true Light," the beloved Son of God, in Whom Father God is well pleased?

DAY 1:   KNOWING HIM

1.   Genesis 1:1,2
In the beginning God created
the heavens   and the earth.
Now the earth was formless   and
empty,   darkness was over
the surface of the deep,   and
the Spirit of God was hovering
over the waters.
Gen. 1:1,2

1.   Genesis 1:1,2
I t b G c
t h   a t e.
N t e w f   a
e,   d w o
t s o t d,   a
t S o G w h
o t w.
Addr.____

2.   Genesis 1:3
And God said,
Let there be light, and
there was light.
Gen. 1:3

2.   Genesis 1:3
A G s,
L t b l, a
t w l.
Addr.____

3.   John 1:9
The true **light** [Jesus] that
gives light
to every man
was coming into the world.
Jn. 1:9

3.   John 1:9
T t l   t
g l
t e m
w c i t w.
Addr.____

4.   John 3:16
For God so loved the world   that
he gave
his one   and only Son,   that
whoever believes in **him** [Jesus]
shall not perish   but
have eternal life.
Jn. 3:16

4.   John 3:16
F G s l t w   t
h g
h o a o S, t
w b i **h**
s n p   b
h e l.
Addr.____

5.   1 Thessalonians 5:9
For God did not appoint us
to suffer wrath   but
to reccive salvation
through
our Lord Jesus Christ.
1 Thess. 5:9

5.   1 Thessalonians 5:9
F G d n a u
t s w   b
t r s
t
o L J C.
Addr.____

DAY 1:   KNOWING HIM

6.   Acts 4:12
Salvation is found
in no one else,
for there is no other name
under heaven ...
by which we must be saved.
Acts 4:12

7.   Hebrews 2:14
Since the children
have flesh   and blood,
[Jesus] **he** too shared
in their humanity   so that
by **his** death
he might destroy him
who holds
the power of death –
that is, the devil –
Heb. 2:14

8.   1 Corinthians 15:21
For since death
came through a man [Adam],
the resurrection of the dead
comes also
through a **man** [Jesus].
1 Cor. 15:21

9.   John 1:4
In **him** was life,   and that
life was the light of men.
Jn. 1:4

10.   Colossians 2:9
For in Christ
all the fullness
of the Deity
lives in bodily form,
Col. 2:9

FOUNDATION SCRIPTURES

6.   Acts 4:12
S i f
i n o e,
f t i n o n
u h ...
b w w m b s.
Addr.____

7.   Hebrews 2:14
S t c
h f   a b,
h t s
i t h   s t
b **h** d
h m d h
w h
t p o d –
t i, t d –
Addr.____

8.   1 Corinthians 15:21
F s d
c t a m,
t r o t d
c a
t a **m**.
Addr.____

9.   John 1:4
I **h** w l,   a t
l w t l o m.
Addr.____

10.   Colossians 2:9
F i C
a t f
o t D
l i b f,
Addr.____

DAY 1:   KNOWING HIM

11.   John 14:6
Jesus answered, I am
the way   and
the truth   and
the life.
No one comes to the Father
except through **me**.
Jn. 14:6

11.   John 14:6
J a, I a
t w   a
t t   a
t l.
N o c t t F
e t **m**.
Addr.____

12.   John 12:46; Luke 2:32
I have come into the world
as a light,   so that
no one who believes in **me**
should stay in darkness. Luke 2:32
a light for revelation
to the Gentiles   and
for glory to ... Israel.
Jn. 12:46; Lk. 2:32

12.   John 12:46; Luke 2:32
I h c i t w
a a l,   s t
n o w b i **m**
s s i d.
a l f r
t t G   a
f g t ... I.
Addr.____

13.   Acts 26:18
to open their eyes   and
turn them from darkness to light,   and
from the power of Satan
to God,   so that
they may receive
forgiveness of sins   and
a place among those who are sanctified
by faith in **me**.
Acts 26:18

13.   Acts 26:18
t o t e   a
t t f d t l, a
f t p o S
t G,   s t
t m r
f o s   a
a p a t w a s
b f i **m**.
Addr.____

14.   Romans 1:20a
For since the creation
of the world
God's invisible qualities –
his eternal power   and
divine nature –
have been clearly seen,
being understood from
what has been made,
Rom. 1:20a

14.   Romans 1:20a
F s t c
o t w
G's i q –
h e p   a
d n –
h b c s,
b u f
w h b m,
Addr.____

15.   John 9:4
As long as it is day ...
[I] must do the work
of **him**
who sent **me**.
Night is coming,
when no one can work.
Jn. 9:4

15.   John 9:4
A l a i i d ...
m d t w
o **h**
w s **m**.
N i c,
w n o c w.
Addr._____

16.   Luke 1:78,79
because of the tender mercy
of our God,
by which the rising sun
will come to us
from heaven to shine
on those living in darkness   and
in the shadow of death,
to guide our feet
into the path of peace.
Lk. 1:78,79

16.   Luke 1:78,79
b o t t m
o o G,
b w t r s
w c t u
f h t s
o t l i d   a
i t s o d,
t g o f
i t p o p.
Addr._____

17.   John 16:33a
I have told you
these things,   so that
in me
you may have peace.
Jn. 16:33a

17.   John 16:33a
I h t y
t t, s t
i m
y m h p.
Addr._____

18.   2 Peter 1:19
And we have the word
of the prophets
made more certain,   and
you will do well
to pay attention to it,
as to a light shining
in a dark place,
until the day dawns   and
the morning star
rises in your hearts.
2 Pet. 1:19

18.   2 Peter 1:19
A w h t w
o t p
m m c,   a
y w d w
t p a t i,
a t a l s
i a d p,
u t d d   a
t m s
r i y h.
Addr._____

19.   Revelation 22:16
I, Jesus ...
I am the Root   and
the Offspring of David,   and
the bright Morning Star.
Rev. 22:16

19.   Revelation 22:16
I, J ...
I a t R   a
t O o D,   a
t b M S.
Addr._____

20.   Matthew 4:16
the people
living in darkness
have seen a great light;
on those living in the land
of the shadow of death
a light
has dawned.
Mt. 4:16

20.   Matthew 4:16
t p
l i d
h s a g l;
o t l i t l
o t s o d
a l
h d.
Addr._____

21.   Matthew 4:17
From that time on
Jesus began to preach,
Repent,
for the kingdom of heaven
is near.
Mt. 4:17

21.   Matthew 4:17
F t t o
J b t p,
R,
f t k o h
i n.
Addr._____

22.   Genesis 1:4
God saw   **that the light**
was good,   and
He separated the light
from the darkness.
Gen. 1:4

22.   Genesis 1:4
G s   **t t l**
w g,   a
H s t l
f t d.
Addr._____

23.   Genesis 1:5
God called the light day,   and
the darkness he called night.   And
there was evening,   and
there was morning –
the first day.
Gen. 1:5

23.   Genesis 1:5
G c t l d,   a
t d h c n.   A
t w e,   a
t w m –
t f d.
Addr._____

DAY TWO: ANALOGY SYNOPSIS

On Creation Day Two,
God's work in Creation was to create expanse –
the firmament or air between heaven and earth.

This reminds me of the crucifixion of Jesus. He was
nailed to the cross and lifted up from the earth. His
death occurred in the air between heaven and earth.

ANALOGY: CREATION DAY TWO

Analogy: a partial likeness between two things that are compared. This analogy seeks to view the Scriptures about Jesus and the church through the narrative of Genesis Chapter One.

Creation Day 2:   Genesis 1:6-8

6 And God said, "Let there be an expanse between the waters to separate water from water." 7 So God made the expanse and separated the water under the expanse from the water above it. And it was so. 8 God called the expanse "sky." And there was evening, and there was morning – the second day.

God's Work in Creation: God created the expanse or firmament/space/air.

Jesus' Work on Earth: Crucifixion: God's penalty of death for sin is paid.

Bible Verse Keywords: Expanse; called the expanse sky; ruler of the kingdom of the air; spiritual forces of evil in heavenly realms; the devil has gone down; serpent; devil; death; (Note: Although Satan is prince of the power of the air, Jesus is King and Lord of all.) Crucify Him; Crucify Him. *Please note the horrific details of the words said, and the deeds done to Jesus prior to His murder.* If you confess with your mouth, Jesus is Lord, and believe in your heart that God raised him from the dead … .

Pondered: 1. "That it was good" is not included in Creation Day Two – the shortest of all the Creation accounts. This curious fact energized my quest of looking for Jesus in Creation. See "The Quest" on page 9.

2. The Bible states in Ephesians 2:2: "the ruler of the kingdom of the air" is Satan. The air is the expanse above the surface of the earth. Reference Job 1:6,7: "One day the angels came to present themselves before the LORD, and Satan also came with them. The LORD said to Satan, 'Where have you come from?' Satan answered the LORD, 'From roaming through the earth and going back and forth in it.'" Satan is the ruler of the kingdom of the air. See "How to be Saved" on page 129.

3. Jesus was crucified in the air. He was lifted up on the cross and hung there until He died. God, His Father, laid His judgement of sin on His Son.

4. The innocent Son chose to do His Father's will. He bore all the sins of the entire world upon His sinless Self before His Holy Father. "Now is the time for judgment on this world; now the prince of this world will be driven out. But I, when I am lifted up from the earth, will draw all men to myself"– John12:31,32. Jesus' work on the cross conquered Satan's power.

5. Jesus was reviled, mocked, spat upon, and tortured by the very humans He created. Then came His anguished separation from His Holy Father.

6. Could it be that Day Two – the shortest account of Creation, in some respect, relates to the inclination for that torturous day to end quickly?

DAY 2:   SAVING FAITH

SALVATION SCRIPTURES

1.   Genesis 1:6-8a
And God said,
Let there be an expanse
        between the waters
        to separate water from water.
So God made the expanse   and
        separated the water
        under the expanse
        from the water above it.   And
        it was so.
God called the expanse sky.
Gen. 1:6-8a

1.   Genesis 1:6-8a
A G s,
L t b a e
    b t w
    t s w f w.
S G m t e   a
    s t w
    u t e
    f t w a i.   A
    i w s.
G c t e s.
Addr.____

2.   Ephesians 2:2b; 6:12
of the ruler
of the kingdom of the air [Satan],
the spirit who is now at work ... Ephesians 6:12
For our struggle
is not against
flesh   and blood,   but
against the rulers,
against the authorities,
against the powers
        of this dark world   and
against the spiritual forces of evil
in the heavenly realms.
Eph. 2:2b; 6:12

2.   Ephesians 2:2b; 6:12
o t r
o t k o t a,
t s w i n a w ...
F o s
i n a
f   a b,   b
a t r,
a t a,
a t p
    o t d w   a
a t s f o e
i t h r.
Addr.____

3.   Revelation 12:12b; 2 Cor. 11:3b
But woe
to the earth   and
the sea,
because the devil
has gone down to you!
He is filled with fury,
because he knows   that
his time is short. 2 Corinthians 11:3b
Eve was deceived
by the serpent's cunning ...
Rev. 12:12b; 2 Cor. 11:3b

3.   Revelation 12:12b; 2 Cor. 11:3b
B w
t t e   a
t s,
b t d
h g d t y!
H i f w f,
b h k   t
h t i s.
E w d
b t s's c ...
Addr.____

4.   Revelation 12:9b; Ephesians 5:6b
that ancient serpent
called the devil,   or Satan,
who leads the whole world astray. Ephesians 5:6b
for because of such things
God's wrath comes on those
who are disobedient.
Rev. 12:9b; Eph. 5:6b

4.   Revelation 12:9b; Ephesians 5:6b
t a s
c t d,   o S,
w l t w w a.
f b o s t
G's w c o t
w a d.
Addr._____

5.   Romans 1:29-32a
They have become filled
with every kind of wickedness,
evil, greed   and depravity.
They are full of envy, murder,
strife, deceit   and malice.
They are gossips, slanderers,
God-haters,
insolent, arrogant   and boastful;
they invent ways of doing evil;
they disobey their parents;
they are senseless, faithless,
heartless, ruthless.
Although they know
God's righteous decree   that
those who do such things
deserve death,
Rom. 1:29-32a

5.   Romans 1:29-32a
T h b f
w e k o w,
e, g   a d.
T a f o e, m,
s, d   a m.
T a g, s,
G-h,
i, a   a b;
t i w o d e;
t d t p;
t a s, f,
h, r.
A t k
G's r d   t
t w d s t
d d,
Addr._____

6.   Romans 6:23a
For the wages of sin
is death,
Rom. 6:23a

6.   Romans 6:23a
F t w o s
i d,
Addr._____

7.   Romans 3:10,11
As it is written: There is
no one   righteous,
not even one;   there is
no one   who understands,
no one   who seeks God.
Rom. 3:10,11

7.   Romans 3:10,11
A i i w: T i
n o   r,
n e o;   t i
n o   w u,
n o   w s G.
Addr._____

DAY 2:   SAVING FAITH

SALVATION SCRIPTURES

8.   1 John 5:19b
the whole world is under
the control of the evil one.
1 Jn. 5:19b

8.   1 John 5:19b
t w w i u
t c o t e o.
Addr._____

9.   Genesis 3:15
[God said to the serpent] And I will put enmity
between you   and the woman,   and
between your offspring   and hers;
he [Jesus] will crush your head,   and
you [serpent/Satan] will strike **his** heel.
Gen. 3:15

9.   Genesis 3:15
A I w p e
b y   a t w, a
b y o a h;
h w c y h,   a
y w s **h** h.
Addr._____

10.   1 John 3:8b
The reason the Son of God
appeared was
to destroy the devil's work.
1 Jn. 3:8b

10.   1 John 3:8b
T r t S o G
a w
t d t d's w.
Addr._____

11.   John 3:19
This is the verdict:
Light has come into the world,   but
men loved darkness instead of light
because their deeds were evil.
Jn. 3:19

11.   John 3:19
T i t v:
L h c i t w, b
m l d i o l
b t d w e.
Addr._____

12.   1 John 2:2
[Jesus] **He** is the atoning sacrifice
for our sins,   and
not only for ours   but also
for the sins
of the whole world
1 Jn. 2:2

12.   1 John 2:2
H i t a s
f o s,   a
n o f o b a
f t s
o t w w
Addr._____

13.   Galatians 3:13
Christ ... becoming a curse for us,
for it is written:
Cursed is everyone
who is hung on a tree.
Gal. 3:13

13.   Galatians 3:13
C ... b a c f u,
f i i w:
C i e
w i h o a t.
Addr._____

DAY 2:   SAVING FAITH

14.   John 12:32,33
[Jesus said] But I, when I am lifted up
from the earth,
will draw all men to **myself**.
He said this to show the kind of death
he was going to die.
Jn. 12:32,33

14.   John 12:32,33
B I, w I a l u
f t e,
w d a m t **m**.
H s t t s t k o d
h w g t d.
Addr._____

15.   Luke 22:3a,4
Then Satan entered Judas ...   And
Judas went to the chief priests   and
the officers of the temple guard   and
discussed with them
how he might betray Jesus.
Lk. 22:3a,4

15.   Luke 22:3a,4
T S e J ...   A
J w t t c p   a
t o o t t g   a
d w t
h h m b J.
Addr._____

16.   John 12:27
[Jesus said] Now **my** heart is troubled,   and
what shall I say?
Father, save **me** from this hour?
No, it was for this very reason
I came to this hour.
Jn. 12:27

16.   John 12:27
N **m** h i t,   a
w s I s?
F, s **m** f t h?
N, i w f t v r
I c t t h.
Addr._____

17.   Mark 14:32a,33b,34a-36
They went to ... Gethsemane ...   and
[Jesus] **he** began to be deeply distressed   and
troubled.
My soul is overwhelmed with sorrow
to the point of death ...
Going a little farther, **he** fell to the ground   and
prayed   that if possible
the hour might pass from **him**.
Abba, Father, **he** said,
everything is possible for **you**.
Take this cup from **me**.
Yet not what I will,   but
what **you** will.
Mk. 14:32a,33b,34a-36

17.   Mark 14:32a,33b,34a-36
T w t ... G ...   a
h b t b d d   a
t.
M s i o w s
t t p o d ...
G a l f, **h** f t t g   a
p   t i p
t h m p f **h**.
A, F, **h** s,
e i p f **y**.
T t c f **m**.
Y n w I w,   b
w **y** w.
Addr._____

18.   Mark 14:41b,42b
[Jesus said] The hour has come.
Look, the Son of Man is betrayed
into the hands of sinners.
Here comes [Judas] **my** betrayer!
Mk. 14:41b,42b

18.   Mark 14:41b,42b
T h h c.
L, t S o M i b
i t h o s.
H c **m** b!
Addr._____

19.   Mark 14:53a,55,56
They took Jesus
to the high priest ...
The chief priests   and
the whole Sanhedrin
were looking for evidence
against Jesus   so that
they could put **him** to death,   but
they did not find any.
Many testified
falsely against **him**,   but
their statements did not agree.
Mk. 14:53a,55,56

19.   Mark 14:53a,55,56
T t J
t t h p ...
T c p   a
t w S
w l f e
a J   s t
t c p **h** t d,   b
t d n f a.
M t
f a **h**,   b
t s d n a.
Addr._____

20.   Luke 22:66,67,70,71
At daybreak the council
of the elders of the people,
both the chief priests   and
teachers of the law,
met together,   and
Jesus was led before them.
If **you** are the Christ,
they said, tell us.
They all asked,
Are **you** then the Son of God?
He replied, You are right
in saying I am.
Then they said,
Why do we need
any more testimony?
We have heard it
from **his** own lips.
Lk. 22:66,67,70,71

20.   Luke 22:66,67,70,71
A d t c
o t e o t p,
b t c p a
t o t l,
m t,   a
J w l b t.
I y a t C,
t s, t u.
T a a,
A y t t S o G?
H r, Y a r
i s I a.
T t s,
W d w n
a m t?
W h h i
f h o l.
Addr._____

21.   Mark 14:64b,65; 15:1b
They all condemned **him**
as worthy of death.
Then some began
to spit at **him**;
they blindfolded **him**,
struck **him** with their fists,   and
said, Prophesy!   And
the guards took **him**   and
beat **him**. Mark 15:1b
They bound Jesus,
led **him** away   and
handed **him** over to Pilate.
Mk. 14:64b,65; 15:1b

21.   Mark 14:64b,65; 15:1b
T a c **h**
a w o d.
T s b
t s a **h**;
t b **h**,
s **h** w t f,   a
s, P!   A
t g t **h**   a
b **h**.
T b J,
l **h** a   a
h **h** o t P.
Addr.____

22.   John 18:37b
You are a king, then! said Pilate.
Jesus answered, You are right
in saying I am a king.
In fact,   for this reason
I was born,   and
for this   I came into the world,
to testify
to the truth.
Jn. 18:37b

22.   John 18:37b
Y a a k, t! s P.
J a, Y a r
i s I a a k.
I f,   f t r
I w b,   a
f t   I c i t w,
t t
t t t.
Addr.____

23.   Mark 15:10,12b-14
[Pilate] knowing it was
out of envy   that
the chief priests had handed Jesus
over to him. ...
What shall I do, then, with the one
you call the king of the Jews?
Pilate asked them.
Crucify **him**! they shouted.
Why? What crime has **he** committed?
asked Pilate.
But they shouted all the louder,
Crucify **him**!
Mk. 15:10,12b-14

23.   Mark 15:10,12b-14
k i w
o o e   t
t c p h h J
o t h. ...
W s I d, t, w t o
y c t k o t J?
P a t.
C **h**! t s.
W? W c h **h** c?
a P.
B t s a t l,
C **h**!
Addr.____

24.   Matthew 27:26b-31

[Pilate] he had Jesus flogged,   and
handed **him** over to be crucified.
Then the governor's soldiers ...
gathered the whole company of soldiers
around **him**.
They stripped **him**   and
put a scarlet robe on **him**,   and
then twisted together
a crown of thorns   and
set it on **his** head.
They put a staff in **his** right hand   and
knelt in front of **him**   and
mocked **him**.
Hail, king of the Jews! they said.
They spit on **him**,   and
took the staff   and
struck **him**   on the head
again   and again.
After they had mocked **him**,
they took off the robe   and
put **his** own clothes on **him**.
Then they led **him** away
to crucify **him**.
Mt. 27:26b-31

24.   Matthew 27:26b-31

h h J f,   a
h **h** o t b c.
T t g's s ...
g t w c o s
a **h**.
T s **h**   a
p a s r o **h**,   a
t t t
a c o t   a
s i o **h** h.
T p a s i **h** r h a
k i f o **h**   a
m **h**.
H, k o t J! t s.
T s o **h**,   a
t t s   a
s **h**   o t h
a   a a.
A t h m **h**,
t t o t r   a
p **h** o c o **h**.
T t l **h** a
t c **h**.
Addr.____

25.   John 19:17

Carrying **his** own cross,
he went out to the place of the Skull
(which in Aramaic is called Golgotha).
Jn. 19:17

25.   John 19:17

C **h** o c,
h w o t t p o t S
(w i A i c G).
Addr.____

26.   Mark 15:31a,32b

... the chief priests   and
the teachers of the law
mocked **him** [Jesus] ...
Those crucified with **him**
also heaped insults on **him**.
Mk. 15:31a,32b

26.   Mark 15:31a,32b

... t c p a
t t o t l
m **h** ...
T c w **h**
a h i o **h**.
Addr.____

27.   Luke 23:34,35a
Jesus said, Father,
forgive them,
for they do not know what
they are doing.   And
they divided up **his** clothes
by casting lots.
The people stood watching,   and
the rulers even sneered at **him**.
Lk. 23:34,35a

27.   Luke 23:34,35a
J s, F,
f t,
f t d n k w
t a d.   A
t d u **h** c
b c l.
T p s w, a
t r e s a **h**.
Addr.____

28.   Luke 23:44,45a
It was now about the sixth hour,   and
darkness came
over the whole land
until the ninth hour,
for the sun stopped shining.
Lk. 23:44,45a

28.   Luke 23:44,45a
I w n a t s h, a
d c
o t w l
u t n h,
f t s s s.
Addr.____

29.   Matthew 27:46
About the ninth hour Jesus
cried out in a loud voice,
Eloi, Eloi, lama sabachthani? –
which means, My God, **my** God,
why have you forsaken **me**?
Mt. 27:46

29.   Matthew 27:46
A t n h J
c o i a l v,
E, E, l s? –
w m, M G, **m** G,
w h y f **m**?
Addr.____

30.   Luke 23:46
Jesus called out with a loud voice,
Father, into **your** hands
I commit **my** spirit.
When **he** had said this,
he breathed **his** last.
Lk. 23:46

30.   Luke 23:46
J c o w a l v,
F, i **y** h
I c **m** s.
W **h** h s t,
h b **h** l.
Addr.____

31.   Mark 15:38
The curtain of the temple
was torn in two
from top   to bottom.
Mk.15:38

31.   Mark 15:38
T c o t t
w t i t
f t   t b.
Addr.____

32.   Genesis 1:8b
And there was evening,   and
there was morning – the second day.
Gen. 1:8b

32.   Genesis 1:8b
A t w e,   a
t w m – t s d.
Addr._____

33.   Romans 10:8,9
But what does it say?   The word is near you;
**it is in your mouth   and
in your heart,   that is,
the word of faith** ... :   **That
if you confess with   your mouth,
Jesus is Lord,   and
believe in your heart   that
God raised him
from the dead,
you will be saved.**
Rom. 10:8,9

33.   Romans 10:8,9
B w d i s?   T w i n y;
i i i y m   a
i y h,   t i,
t w o f ... :   T
i y c w   y m,
J i L,   a
b i y h   t
G r h
f t d,
y w b s.
Addr._____

34.   Matthew 12:40
For as Jonah   was three days   and
three nights   in the belly of a huge fish,
so the Son of Man   will be three days   and
three nights   in the heart of the earth.
Mt. 12:40

34.   Matthew 12:40
F a J   w t d   a
t n   i t b o a h f,
s t S o M   w b t d   a
t n   i t h o t e.
Addr._____

35.   Romans 10:17
**Consequently, faith comes from hearing
the message,   and
the message is heard
through the word of Christ.**
Rom. 10:17

35.   Romans 10:17
C, f c f h
t m,   a
t m i h
t t w o C.
Addr._____

36.   Hebrews 11:6
And without faith
it is impossible to please God,
because anyone who comes to **him**
must believe that **he** exists   and that
he rewards those
who earnestly seek **him**.
Heb. 11:6

36.   Hebrews 11:6
A w f
i i i t p G,
b a w c t **h**
m b t **h** c   a t
h r t
w e s **h**.
Addr._____

DAY THREE: ANALOGY SYNOPSIS

On Creation Day Three,
God's work in Creation was to create dry ground or
earth, and the first living organisms – plant life.

This reminds me of the burial of Jesus in the earth. The
third day, He is the firstfruit living – resurrected life.

ANALOGY: CREATION DAY THREE

Analogy: a partial likeness between two things that are compared. This analogy seeks to view the Scriptures about Jesus and the church through the narrative of Genesis Chapter One.

Creation Day 3: Genesis 1:9-12

9 And God said, "Let the water under the sky be gathered to one place, and let dry ground appear." And it was so. 10 God called the dry ground "land," and the gathered waters he called "seas." And God saw that it was good. 11 Then God said, "Let the land produce vegetation: seed-bearing plants and trees on the land that bear fruit with seed in it, according to their various kinds." And it was so. 12 The land produced vegetation: plants bearing seed according to their kinds and trees bearing fruit with seed in it according to their kinds. And God saw that it was good. 13 And there was evening, and there was morning – the third day.

God's Work in Creation: Dry ground (earth), seas, and vegetation are created on the third day.

Jesus' Work on Earth: Burial and Resurrection: Dry land earth and vegetation are essential to Jesus' burial. He is buried in the earth, and He is risen on the third day.

Bible Verse Keywords: Dry ground land; herb; seed-bearing; trees; bear fruit with seed in it; fruit with seed in it according their kinds; the third day; myrrh; aloes; linen; spices; bury; garden; tomb cut out of the rock; buried; third day; firstfruits; made alive; resurrection and the life; will live; the firstfruits of those who ... sleep; the benefit you reap leads to holiness; eternal life.

Pondered: 1. The body of Jesus is prepared for burial with a variety of vegetation: a mixture of myrrh (a gum resin from small, spiny trees) and aloes (plant leaves with a bitter juice); and His body is bound with strips of linen (cloth from flax plants) with spices (aromatic substances from plants).

2. The body of Jesus is placed in a new tomb cut out of rock (the hard part of the earth's crust). The tomb is in a garden (a place of cultivated vegetation). Thus Jesus was laid in a garden, in a tomb, in the earth.

3. God particularly notes "trees on the land that bear fruit with seed in it." 1 Corinthians 15:20a says, "But Christ has indeed been raised from the dead, the firstfruits" of those who died trusting in Him. James 1:18 states, "He [Jesus Christ] chose to give us birth through the word of truth, that we might be a kind of firstfruits of all he created."

4. On the third day, the first living organisms of plant life are created. On the third day, Jesus is the firstfruit living the eternally resurrected life.

5. "And God saw that it was good," is declared twice. It is first said for dry land and Seas, and again after the creation of plants – the first earth life.

6. Could be that "good" declared twice brings to mind the Father's joy of: first seeing His Son's body off the cross and buried in the earth, and again after seeing His Son alive – the first resurrected life?

1.   Genesis 1:9,10
And God said,
Let the water under the sky
be gathered to one place,   and
let dry ground appear.   And
it was so.
God called the dry ground land,   and
the gathered waters
he called seas.   **And**
God saw that it was good.
Gen. 1:9,10

2.   Genesis 1:11
Then God said,
Let the land
produce vegetation:
seed-bearing plants   and
trees on the land   that
bear fruit with seed in it,
according to their various kinds.   And
it was so.
Gen. 1:11

3.   John 19:38b-40
Now Joseph [of Arimathaea] was
a disciple of Jesus ...
he came   and
took the body away.
He was accompanied by Nicodemus ...
Nicodemus brought a mixture
of myrrh   and aloes,
about seventy-five pounds.
Taking Jesus' body,
the two of them wrapped **it**,
with the spices,
in strips of linen.
This was in accordance with
Jewish burial customs.
Jn. 19:38b-40

1.   Genesis 1:9,10
A G s,
L t w u t s
b g t o p,   a
l d g a.   A
i w s.
G c t d g l, a
t g w
h c s.   **A**
G s t i w g.
Addr._____

2.   Genesis 1:11
T G s,
L t l
p v:
s-b p   a
t o t l   t
b f w s i i,
a t t v k.   A
i w s.
Addr._____

3.   John 19:38b-40
N J w
a d o J ...
h c   a
t t b a.
H w a b N ...
N b a m
o m   a a,
a s-f p.
T J' b,
t t o t w **i**,
w t s,
i s o l.
T w i a w
J b c.
Addr._____

DAY 3:   STANDING SECURE

ASSURANCE SCRIPTURES

4.   John 19:41,42; Matthew 27:60b
At the place
where Jesus was crucified,
there was a garden,   and
in the garden a new tomb ... Matthew 27:60b
cut out of the rock ... John 19:41b,42
in which no one had ever been laid.
Because it was
the Jewish day of Preparation   and
since the tomb was nearby,
they laid Jesus there.
Jn. 19:41,42; Mt. 27:60b

4.   John 19:41,42; Matthew 27:60b
A t p
w J w c,
t w a g,   a
i t g a n t ...
c o o t r ...
i w n o h e b l.
B i w
t J d o P a
s t t w n,
t l J t.
Addr._____

5.   1 Corinthians 15:1,2a-4
Now, brothers,   I want to remind you
of the gospel ...   which you received   and
on which   you have taken your stand.
By this gospel   you are saved,
if   you hold firmly to the word
I preached to   you.
Otherwise,   you have believed in vain.
For what I received I passed on to you
as of first importance: that
Christ died for our sins
according to the Scriptures,   that
he was buried,   that
he was raised on the third day
according to the Scriptures,
1 Cor. 15:1,2a-4

5.   1 Corinthians 15:1,2a-4
N, b,   I w t r y
o t g ...   w y r   a
o w   y h t y s.
B t g   y a s,
i   y h f t t w
I p t   y.
O,   y h b i v.
F w I r I p o t y
a o f i: t
C d f o s
a t t S,   t
h w b,   t
h w r o t t d
a t t S,
Addr._____

6.   Matthew 28:1a,5b,6a
After the Sabbath, at dawn
on the first day of the week ...
The angel said ... for I know   that
you are looking for Jesus,
who was crucified.
He is not here;
he has risen,
just as **he** said.
Mt. 28:1a,5b,6a

6.   Matthew 28:1a,5b,6a
A t S, a d
o t f d o t w ...
T a s ... f I k   t
y a l f J,
w w c.
H i n h;
h h r,
j a **h** s.
Addr._____

DAY 3:   STANDING SECURE

ASSURANCE SCRIPTURES

7.   Genesis 1:12a
The land produced vegetation:
plants bearing seed
according to their kinds   and
trees bearing fruit
with seed in it
according to their kinds.
Gen. 1:12a

7.   Genesis 1:12a
T l p v:
p b s
a t t k   a
t b f
w s i i
a t t k.
Addr.____

8.   1 Corinthians 15:20,21
But Christ has indeed
been raised from the dead,
the firstfruits of those
who have fallen asleep.
For since death came
through a man [Adam],
the resurrection of the dead
comes also
through a **man** [Jesus].
1 Cor. 15:20,21

8.   1 Corinthians 15:20,21
B C h i
b r f t d,
t f o t
w h f a.
F s d c
t a m,
t r o t d
c a
t a **m**.
Addr.____

9.   1 Corinthians 15:22,23
For as in Adam all die,
so in Christ
all will be made alive.   But
each in his own turn:
Christ, the firstfruits;
then, when **he** comes,
those who belong to **him**.
1 Cor. 15:22,23

9.   1 Corinthians 15:22,23
F a i A a d,
s i C
a w b m a.   B
e i h o t:
C, t f;
t, w **h** c,
t w b t **h**.
Addr.____

10.   John 11:25
Jesus said ...
I am the resurrection   and
the life.
He who believes in **me**
will live,
even though he dies;
Jn. 11:25

10.   John 11:25
J s ...
I a t r   a
t l.
H w b i **m**
w l,
e t h d;
Addr.____

11.   Acts 2:30,31
But [King David] he was a prophet   and
knew   that God had promised him
on oath   that
he [God] would place
one of his [King David's] descendants
on his throne.
Seeing what was ahead,
he spoke of
the resurrection of the Christ,   that
he was not abandoned
to the grave,   nor
did **his** body see decay.
Acts 2:30,31

11.   Acts 2:30,31
B h w a p   a
k   t G h p h
o o   t
h w p
o o h d
o h t.
S w w a,
h s o
t r o t C,   t
h w n a
t t g,   n
d **h** b s d.
Addr._____

12.   Acts 13:37,38
But the one **whom** God
raised from the dead
did not see decay.
Therefore, my brothers,
I want you to know   that
through Jesus
the forgiveness of sins
is proclaimed to you.
Acts 13:37,38

12.   Acts 13:37,38
B t o **w** G
r f t d
d n s d.
T, m b,
I w y t k   t
t J
t f o s
i p t y.
Addr._____

13.   Romans 6:22,23
But now   that
you have been set free from sin   and
have become slaves to God,
the benefit you reap
leads to holiness,   and
the result is eternal life.
For the wages of sin
is death,   but
the gift of God
is eternal life
in Christ Jesus our Lord.
Rom. 6:22,23

13.   Romans 6:22,23
B n   t
y h b s f f s a
h b s t G,
t b y r
l t h,   a
t r i e l.
F t w o s
i d,   b
t g o G
i e l
i C J o L.
Addr._____

Memorizing God's Word:™ HIStory © (NIV)   R. M. Lewis   67

DAY 3:   STANDING SECURE

ASSURANCE SCRIPTURES

14.   Ephesians 2:4,5a,8,9
But because of **his** great love for us,
God, **who** is rich in mercy,
made us alive   with Christ
even when we were   dead in transgressions ...
For it is by grace   you have been saved,
through faith –   and
this not from yourselves,
it is the gift of God –
not by works,   so that
no one can boast.
Eph. 2:4,5a,8,9

14.   Ephesians 2:4,5a,8,9
B b o **h** g l f u,
G, **w** i r i m,
m u a   w C
e w w w   d i t ...
F i i b g   y h b s,
t f –   a
t n f y,
i i t g o G –
n b w,   s t
n o c b.
Addr._____

15.   1 John 2:1; 1:9
My dear children, I write this to you
so that you will not sin.   But
if anybody does sin,
we have one
who speaks to the Father
in our defense –
Jesus Christ,
the Righteous One. 1 John 1:9
If we confess our sins,
he is faithful   and just and
will forgive us our sins   and
purify us from all unrighteousness.
1 Jn. 2:1; 1:9

15.   1 John 2:1; 1:9
M d c, I w t t y
s t y w n s.   B
i a d s,
w h o
w s t t F
i o d –
J C,
t R O.
I w c o s,
h i f   a j a
w f u o s   a
p u f a u.
Addr._____

16.   Psalm 15:1b,2
Who may live on **your** holy hill?
He whose walk is blameless   and
who does what is righteous,
who speaks the truth from his heart
Ps. 15:1b,2

16.   Psalm 15:1b,2
W m l o **y** h h?
H w w i b   a
w d w i r,
w s t t f h h
Addr._____

17.   Genesis 1:12b,13
And God saw that it was good.   And
there was evening,   and
there was morning – the third day.
Gen. 1:12b,13

17.   Genesis 1:12b,13
A G s t i w g.   A
t w e,   a
t w m – t t d.
Addr._____

DAY FOUR: ANALOGY SYNOPSIS

On Creation Day Four,
God's work in Creation was to make lights. He made two great lights and the stars also. These created lights bring light to the earth imitating the unique light of Creation Day One.

This reminds me of the prophets and the apostles Jesus commissioned to be His witnesses. These created beings bring light to the earth imitating the True Light, Who returned to His Father.

ANALOGY: CREATION DAY FOUR

Analogy: a partial likeness between two things that are compared. This analogy seeks to view the Scriptures about Jesus and the church through the narrative of Genesis Chapter One.

Creation Day 4: Genesis 1:14-19

14 And God said, "Let there be lights in the expanse of the sky to separate the day from the night, and let them serve as signs to mark seasons and days and years, 15 and let them be lights in the expanse of the sky to give light on the earth." And it was so. 16 God made two great lights – the greater light to govern the day and the lesser light to govern the night. He also made the stars. 17 God set them in the expanse of the sky to give light on the earth, 18 to govern the day and the night, and to separate light from darkness. And God saw that it was good. 19 And there was evening, and there was morning – the fourth day.

God's Work in Creation: God made two great lights, and He made the stars also.

Jesus' Work on Earth: Witnesses: The resurrected Jesus Christ appeared to His apostles. Christ commissioned them to be His witnesses, but they were told to wait for the Holy Spirit. (Pentecost has not come.) Jesus Christ returned to heaven.

Bible Verse Keywords: Lights; day; night; signs; seasons; days; years; true light; his witnesses; let your light shine; stay in the city; was taken into heaven; put your trust in the light; become sons of light; all the prophets testify; a witness to testify concerning that light; two great lights; greater light to govern the day; lesser light to govern the night; great cloud of witnesses; stars of the sky; no one greater than; least of the apostles; sinners, of whom I am the worst; less than the least; his witnesses; our citizenship is in heaven; to give light on the earth.

Pondered: 1. It is the resurrection of Christ that secures the resurrection of believers. 1 Corinthians 15:13,14 states, "If there is no resurrection of the dead, then not even Christ has been raised. And if Christ has not been raised, our preaching is useless and so is your faith." Abraham, King David, all the prophets, and the apostles are some of the "cloud of witnesses" who are sons of His resurrection, sons of the Light, and His lights on earth.

2. God has an order for His church. God states that He appointed to the church – first apostles and second prophets. Of the prophets, Jesus said that John the Baptist was the greatest of all. John came as the testifying witness of the Light, and said that Jesus must increase and I must decrease. Jesus declares that whoever is least in the kingdom of God is greater than John the Baptist. Apostle Paul identifies himself as "less than the least."

3. God first appointed apostles to the church. Of the twelve apostles, it is difficult to think of a more humble and influential apostle than Apostle Paul. He is the "foremost interpreter of Christ through all the ages."MSB NAS

4. Could it be that on Creation Day Four those "made lights" that God set in the expanse are His witnesses on earth – citizens of heaven and His lights on the earth?

DAY 4:   BECOMING CHRISTLIKE   TRANSFORMATION SCRIPTURES

1.   Genesis 1:14
And God said, Let there be lights
in the expanse of the sky
to separate the day from the night,   and
let them serve as signs to mark seasons   and
days and years,
Gen. 1:14

1.   Genesis 1:14
A G s, L t b l
i t e o t s
t s t d f t n,   a
l t s a s t m s   a
d a y,
Addr.____

2.   1 Peter 1:20a; John 1:9a; Acts 13:30
[Jesus] He was chosen before
the creation of the world,   but
was revealed in these last times John 1:9a
The true **light** Acts 13:30
... God raised **him** from the dead,
1 Pet. 1:20a; Jn. 1:9a; Acts 13:30

2.   1 Pet. 1:20a; John 1:9a; Acts 13:30
H w c b
t c o t w,   b
w r i t l t
T t l
... G r h f t d,
Addr.____

3.   Acts 1:3
After **his** suffering,
[Jesus] **he** showed **himself** ...   and
gave many convincing proofs   that
he was alive.
He appeared to them
over a period of forty days   and
spoke about the kingdom of God.
Acts 1:3

3.   Acts 1:3
A **h** s,
h s **h** ...   a
g m c p   t
h w a.
H a t t
o a p o f d   a
s a t k o G.
Addr.____

4.   Acts 13:31
and for many days **he** was seen
by those who had traveled with **him**
from Galilee to Jerusalem.
They arc now **his** witnesses
to our people.
Acts 13:31

4.   Acts 13:31
a f m d **h** w s
b t w h t w **h**
f G t J.
T a n **h** w
t o p.
Addr.____

5.   Luke 24:36b
Jesus **himself** stood
among them   and
said to them,
Peace be with you.
Lk. 24:36b

5.   Luke 24:36b
J **h** s
a t   a
s t t,
P b w y.
Addr.____

6.   Luke 24:39,45
[Jesus said] Look at **my** hands and
my feet.
It is I **myself**!
Touch **me**   and see;
a ghost does not have
flesh   and bones,
as you see I have.
Then **he** opened their minds
so they could understand
the Scriptures.
Lk. 24:39,45

6.   Luke 24:39,45
L a **m** h   a
m f.
I i I **m**!
T **m**   a s;
a g d n h
f   a b,
a y s I h.
T **h** o t m
s t c u
t S.
Addr._____

7.   John 15:27
And you [apostles] also must testify,
for you have been with **me**
from the beginning.
Jn. 15:27

7.   John 15:27
A y a m t,
f y h b w **m**
f t b.
Addr._____

8.   Matthew 5:16
In the same way,
let your light shine
before men,   that
they may see your good deeds   and
praise your Father in heaven.
Mt. 5:16

8.   Matthew 5:16
I t s w,
l y l s
b m,   t
t m s y g d   a
p y F i h.
Addr._____

9.   Luke 24:49b; Mark 16:19
[Jesus said] but stay in the city
until you have been clothed
with power from on high. Mark 16:19
After the Lord Jesus
had spoken to them,

he was taken up
into heaven   and
he sat
at the right hand
of God.
Lk. 24:49b; Mk. 16:19

9.   Luke 24:49b; Mark 16:19
b s i t c
u y h b c
w p ſ o h.
A t L J
h s t t,

h w t u
i h   a
h s
a t r h
o G.
Addr._____

10.   Genesis 1:15
[God said] and let them be lights
in the expanse of the sky
to give light on the earth.   And it was so.
Gen. 1:15

10.   Genesis 1:15
a l t b l
i t e o t s
t g l o t e.   A i w s.
Addr.____

11.   John 12:36a
Put your trust in the **light** [Jesus]
while you have it,   so that
you may become sons of light.
Jn. 12:36a

11.   John 12:36a
P y t i t **l**
w y h i,   s t
y m b s o l.
Addr.____

12.   Ecclesiastes 3:1
There is a time   for everything,   and
a season for   every activity under heaven:
Eccl. 3:1

12.   Ecclesiastes 3:1
T i a t   f e,   a
a s f   e a u h:
Addr.____

13.   1 Peter 1:20a; Acts 10:43
[Jesus] He was chosen
before the creation of the world ... Acts 10:43
All the prophets testify about **him**   that
everyone
who believes in **him**
receives forgiveness of sins
through **his** name.
1 Pet. 1:20a; Acts 10:43

13.   1 Peter 1:20a; Acts 10:43
H w c
b t c o t w ...
A t p t a **h**   t
e
w b i **h**
r f o s
t **h** n.
Addr.____

14.   Hebrews 12:1b; Isaiah 61:1,2a
we are surrounded by
such a great cloud of witnesses ... Isaiah. 61:1,2a
[Isaiah prophesied Jesus] The Spirit of
the Sovereign LORD   is on **me**,
because the LORD   has anointed **me**
to preach good news   to the poor.
He has sent **me**   to bind up the brokenhearted,
to proclaim freedom   for the captives and
release from darkness   for the prisoners,
to proclaim the year
of the LORD's favor ...
Heb. 12:1b; Is. 61:1,2a

14.   Hebrews 12:1b; Isaiah 61:1,2a
w a s b
s a g c o w ...
T S o
t S L   i o **m**,
b t L   h a **m**
t p g n   t t p.
H h s **m**   t b u t b,
t p f   f t c   a
r f d   f t p,
t p t y
o t L's f ...
Addr.____

15.   John 1:23,7,8; 3:30; Daniel 4:3a
John [the Baptist] replied in the words
of Isaiah the prophet,
I am the voice of one
calling in the desert,
Make straight the way for the Lord. John 1:7,8
He came as a witness to testify
concerning that **light** [Jesus],   so that
through him all men might believe.
He himself was not the **light**;
he came only as   a witness to the **light**. John 3:30
He [Jesus] must become greater;
I [John] must become less. Dan. 4:3a
How great are **his** signs ...
Jn. 1:23,7,8; 3:30; Dan. 4:3a

15.   John 1:23,7,8; 3:30; Daniel 4:3a
J r i t w
o I t p,
I a t v o o
c i t d,
M s t w f t L.
H c a a w t t
c t **l**,   s t
t h a m m b.
H h w n t **l**;
h c o a   a w t t **l**.
H m b g;
I m b **l**.
H g a **h** s ...
Addr._____

16.   Genesis 1:16
God made   two great lights –
the greater light   to govern the day   and
the lesser light   to govern the night.
He also made the stars.
Gen. 1:16

16.   Genesis 1:16
G m   t g l –
t g l   t g t d   a
t l l   t g t n.
H a m t s.
Addr._____

17.   Hebrews 12:1b; Genesis 26:4
such a great cloud of witnesses ...   Genesis 26:4
[God said to Abraham] I will make
your descendants as numerous as
the stars in the sky   and
will give them all these lands,   and
through your offspring
all nations on earth will be blessed,
Heb. 12:1b; Gen. 26:4

17.   Hebrews 12:1b; Genesis 26:4
s a g c o w ...
I w m
y d a n a
t s i t s   a
w g t a t l,   a
t y o
a n o e w b b,
Addr._____

18.   Galatians 3:16
The promises were spoken
to Abraham   and to his seed.
The Scripture does not say   and to sccds,
meaning many people, but   and to your seed,
meaning one person,   **who** is Christ.
Gal. 3:16

18.   Galatians 3:16
T p w s
t A   a t h s.
T S d n s   a t s,
m m p, b   a t y s,
m o p,   **w** i C.
Addr._____

DAY 4:   BECOMING CHRISTLIKE   TRANSFORMATION SCRIPTURES

19.   1 Corinthians 12:28a
And in the church
God has appointed

first of all apostles,
second prophets ...
1 Cor. 12:28a

19.   1 Corinthians 12:28a
A i t c
G h a

f o a a,
s p ...
Addr._____

20.   Luke 7:28
[Jesus said] I tell you,
among those born of women
there is no one greater
than John [the Baptist];

yet the one who is least
in the kingdom of God
is greater than he.
Lk. 7:28

20.   Luke 7:28
I t y,
a t b o w
t i n o g
t J;

y t o w i l
i t k o G
i g t h.
Addr._____

21.   1 Corinthians 15:9,10a
[Paul said] For I am

the least of the apostles   and
do not even deserve
to be called an apostle,
because I persecuted
the church of God.   But
by the grace of God
I am what I am,   and
his grace to me
was not without effect.
1 Cor. 15:9,10a

21.   1 Corinthians 15:9,10a
F I a

t l o t a   a
d n e d
t b c a a,
b I p
t c o G.   B
b t g o G
I a w I a, a
h g t m
w n w e.
Addr._____

22.   1 Timothy 1:15b
Christ Jesus came
into the world
to save sinners –

of whom I am the worst.
1 Tim. 1:15b

22.   1 Timothy 1:15b
C J c
i t w
t s s –

o w I a t w.
Addr._____

23.   Ephesians 3:8
Although I am

less than the least of
all God's people,
this grace was given me:
to preach to the Gentiles
the unsearchable riches of Christ,
Eph. 3:8

23.   Ephesians 3:8
A I a

l t t l o
a G's p,
t g w g m:
t p t t G
t u r o C,
Addr._____

24.   Acts 10:42
[Jesus] He commanded us [apostles]
to preach to the people   and
to testify   that
he is the one
whom God appointed as judge
of the living   and
the dead.
Acts 10:42

24.   Acts 10:42
H c u
t p t t p   a
t t   t
h i t o
w G a a j
o t l   a
t d.
Addr._____

25.   Acts 5:32a; Philippians 3:20
We are witnesses of these things ... Phil. 3:20
But our citizenship is in heaven.   And
we eagerly await a Savior from there,
the Lord Jesus Christ,
Acts 5:32a; Phil. 3:20

25.   Acts 5:32a; Philippians 3:20
W a w o t t ...
B o c i i h.   A
w e a a S f t,
t L J C,
Addr._____

26.   Genesis 1:17-19
God set them
in the expanse of the sky
to give light on the earth,
to govern the day   and
the night,   and
to separate light from darkness. **And**

God saw that it was good.   And
there was evening,   and
there was morning –
the fourth day.
Gen. 1:17-19

26.   Genesis 1:17-19
G s t
i t e o t s
t g l o t e,
t g t d   a
t n,   a
t s l f d.   **A**

G s t i w g. A
t w e,   a
t w m –
t f d.
Addr._____

DAY FIVE: ANALOGY SYNOPSIS

On Creation Day Five,
God's work in Creation was to create a new
kind of life – flesh and blood water creatures,
generally called fish, and afterwards birds that
fly above the earth.

This reminds me of Christ creating a new life
in the flesh and blood apostles – fishers of men,
and afterwards recipients of the Holy Spirit, Who
often is symbolically represented as a dove
flying above the earth.

ANALOGY: CREATION DAY FIVE

Analogy: a partial likeness between two things that are compared. This analogy seeks to view the Scriptures about Jesus and the church through the narrative of Genesis Chapter One.

Creation Day 5: Genesis 1:20-23

20 And God said, "Let the water teem with living creatures, and let birds fly above the earth across the expanse of the sky." 21 So God created the great creatures of the sea and every living and moving thing with which the water teems, according to their kinds, and every winged bird according to its kind. And God saw that it was good. 22 God blessed them and said, "Be fruitful and increase in number and fill the water in the seas, and let the birds increase on the earth." 23 And there was evening, and there was morning – the fifth day.

God's Work in Creation: Water creatures, generally called fish, and then birds are created.

Jesus' Work on Earth: Great Commission and Pentecost: The apostles submitting to the new command to love others, are in one accord. Thereby the Holy Spirit comes.

Bible Verse Keywords: Water teem with living creatures; birds fly above; A new command I give you: love one another; I have loved you; new creation; make you fishers of men; came by water and blood; the Holy Spirit descended on him in bodily form like a dove; unless one is born of water and the Spirit; The Spirit gives life; the flesh counts for nothing; Go and make disciples of all nations; filled with the Holy Spirit; the one who is in you is greater than one who is in the world; the Lord added to their number daily; Whoever loves God must also love his brother; leaving you an example; Christ's ambassadors; ministry of reconciliation.

Pondered:

1. All kinds of sea creatures, generally called fish, are created and live in peace. Commissioned by Jesus as fishers of men and living out the new love commandment, the disciples live in peace awaiting the Holy Spirit.

2. God created birds. The dove is often symbolic of the Holy Spirit. At Pentecost the Holy Spirit comes to indwell the disciples with power.

3. On Day Five, God created new living creations – unlike plant life. These are flesh and blood water creatures, and afterwards birds. Jesus gave a new life to the flesh and blood apostles. They were born again, baptized, and afterwards filled with the Holy Spirit. Christ created new living creations of spiritual life – unlike natural life.

4. Some of the water creatures are mammals; their offspring will be born. Thus waters teem with a multitude of fish. After Pentecost Peter, a fisher of men, preaches the gospel and thousands from every nation are born again. Thus waters teemed with a multitude of believers being baptized.

5. Could it be that God's sequence of creating fish, and afterwards birds, mirrors the sequence of commissioning the fishers of men, and afterwards giving them the Holy Spirit (often depicted as a dove)?

DAY 5: GLORIFYING GOD

1.   Genesis 1:20
And God said,
Let the water teem
with living creatures,   and

let birds fly above the earth
across the expanse of the sky.
Gen. 1:20

1.   Genesis 1:20
A G s,
L t w t
w l c,   a

l b f a t e
a t e o t s.
Addr._____

2.   John 13:34a,35a
[Jesus said] A new command
I give you:
Love one another.
As I have loved you ...
By this
all mcn will know   that
you are **my** disciples,
Jn. 13:34a,35a

2.   John 13:34a,35a
A n c
I g y:
L o a.
A I h l y ...
B t
a m w k   t
y a **m** d,
Addr._____

3.   2 Corinthians 5:17; Mark 1:17
Therefore, if anyone is in Christ,
he is a new creation;
the old has gone,
the new has come! Mark 1:17
Come, follow **me**, Jesus said,   and
I will make you
fishers of men.
2 Cor. 5:17; Mk. 1:17

3.   2 Corinthians 5:17; Mark 1:17
T, i a i i C,
h i a n c;
t o h g,
t n h c!
C, f **m**, J s, a
I w m y
f o m.
Addr._____

4.   1 John 5:6
[Jesus] This is the one **who** came
by water and blood –
Jesus Christ.
He did not come by water only,   but
by water   and blood.   And
it is the Spirit
who testifies,
because the Spirit
is the truth.
1 Jn. 5:6

4.   1 John 5:6
T i t o w c
b w a b –
J C.
H d n c b w o, b
b w   a b.   A
i i t S
w t,
b t S
i t t.
Addr._____

5.   Luke 3:21b,22
Jesus was baptized too ...
heaven was opened   and
the Holy Spirit   descended on **him**

in bodily form   like a dove.   And
a voice   came from heaven:
You are **my** Son,   **whom** I love;
with **you**   I am well pleased.
Lk. 3:21b,22

5.   Luke 3:21b,22
J w b t ...
h w o   a
t H S   d o **h**

i b f   l a d.   A
a **v**   c f h:
Y a **m** S,   **w** I l;
w **y**   I a w p.
Addr._____

6.   John 3:5b; 1 John 5:1a
[Jesus said] no one can enter
the kingdom of God unless
he is born of water   and
the Spirit. 1 John 5:1a
Everyone who believes   that
Jesus is the Christ
is born of God,
Jn. 3:5b; 1 Jn. 5:1a

6.   John 3:5b; 1 John 5:1a
n o c e
t k o G u
h i b o w   a
t S.
E w b   t
J i t C
i b o G,
Addr._____

7.   John 3:3,5b
Jesus declared, I tell you the truth,
no one can see
the kingdom of God
unless he is born again.
no one can enter
the kingdom of God
unless he is born of water   and
the Spirit.
Jn. 3:3,5b

7.   John 3:3,5b
J d, I t y t t,
n o c s
t k o G
u h i b a.
n o c e
t k o G
u h i b o w   a
t S.
Addr._____

8.   John 6:63
The Spirit gives life;
the flesh counts for
nothing.
The words I have spoken to you
are spirit   and
they are life.
Jn. 6:63

8.   John 6:63
T S g l;
t f c f
n.
T w I h s t y
a s   a
t a l.
Addr._____

9.   Mark 16:15; Matthew 28:18,19
[Jesus] He said to them,
Go into all the world   and
preach the good news
to all creation. Matthew 28:18,19
... Jesus came to them   and said,
All authority in heaven   and on earth
has been given   to **me**.
Therefore go   and
make disciples   of all nations,
baptizing them in the name
of the Father   and
of the Son   and
of the Holy Spirit,
Mk. 16:15; Mt. 28:18,19

9.   Mark 16:15; Matthew 28:18,19
H s t t,
G i a t w   a
p t g n
t a c.
... J c t t   a s,
A a i h   a o e
h b g   t **m**.
T g   a
m d   o a n,
b t i t n
o t F   a
o t S   a
o t H S,
Addr._____

10.   Acts 1:4b,5
[Jesus] **he** gave them this command:
Do not leave Jerusalem,   but
wait for the gift   **my** Father promised,
which you have heard **me**   speak about.
For John baptized with water,   but
in a few days you will be baptized
with the Holy Spirit.
Acts 1:4b,5

10.   Acts 1:4b,5
h g t t c:
D n l J,   b
w f t g   **m** F p,
w y h h **m**   s a.
F J b w w,   b
i a f d y w b b
w t H S.
Addr._____

11.   Acts 2:1,2,4; 4:31b
When the day of Pentecost came,
they were all together in one place.
Suddenly a sound like
the blowing of a violent wind
came from heaven   and
filled the whole house
where they were sitting.
All of them were filled with
the Holy Spirit   and
began to speak in other tongues
as the Spirit enabled them.   And
they ... spoke the word of God boldly.
Acts 2:1,2,4; 4:31b

11.   Acts 2:1,2,4; 4:31b
W t d o P c,
t w a t i o p.
S a s l
t b o a v w
c f h   a
f t w h
w t w s.
A o t w f w
t H S   a
b t s i o t
a t S e t.   A
t ... s t w o G b.
Addr._____

12.   Acts 2:38
Peter replied [to the multitude from every nation],
Repent   and
be baptized, every one of you,
in the name of Jesus Christ
for the forgiveness of your sins.   And
you will receive
the gift
of the Holy Spirit.
Acts 2:38

12.   Acts 2:38
P r,
R   a
b b, e o o y,
i t n o J C
f t f o y s.   A
y w r
t g
o t H S.
Addr._____

13.   Acts 2:41,47b
Those who accepted his message
were baptized,   and
about three thousand were added
to their number that day.   And
the Lord added
to their number daily
those who were being saved.
Acts 2:41,47b

13.   Acts 2:41,47b
T w a h m
w b,   a
a t t w a
t t n t d.   A
t L a
t t n d
t w w b s.
Addr._____

14.   1 John 4:4
You, dear children, are from God   and
have overcome them,
because the one **who** is in you
is greater
than the one who is in the world.
1 Jn. 4:4

14.   1 John 4:4
Y, d c, a f G   a
h o t,
b t o w i i y
i g
t t o w i i t w.
Addr.____

15.   1 Corinthians 2:9,10
However, as it is written:
No eye has seen,   no ear has heard,
no mind has conceived
what God has prepared for those
who love **him** –   but
God has revealed it to us
by **his** Spirit.
The Spirit searches all things,
even the deep things of God.
1 Cor. 2:9,10

15.   1 Corinthians 2:9,10
H, a i i w:
N e h s,   n e h h,
n m h c
w G h p f t
w l **h** –   b
G h r i t u
b **h** S.
T S s a t,
e t d t o G.
Addr._____

DAY 5:   GLORIFYING GOD

MATURATION SCRIPTURES

16.   1 John 4:20,21; 2:5
If anyone says,   I love God,
yet hates his brother,
he is a liar.
For anyone who does not love
his brother,
whom he has seen,
cannot love God,
whom he has not seen.   And
he has given us this command:
Whoever loves God
must also love his brother.   But
if anyone obeys **his** word,
God's love is truly
made complete in him.
This is how we know
we are in **him**:
1 Jn. 4:20,21; 2:5

16.   1 John 4:20,21; 2:5
I a s,   I l G,
y h h b,
h i a l.
F a w d n l
h b,
w h h s,
c l G,
w h h n s.   A
h h g u t c:
W l G
m a l h b.   B
i a o **h** w,
G's l i t
m c i h.
T i h w k
w a i **h**:
Addr._____

17.   1 Peter 2:23
When they hurled
their insults at **him**,
he did not retaliate;
when **he** suffered,
he made no threats.
Instead, **he** entrusted **himself**
to **him** [Father God]
who judges justly.
1 Pet. 2:23

17.   1 Peter 2:23
W t h
t i a **h**,
h d n r;
w **h** s,
h m n t.
I, **h** e **h**
t **h**
w j j.
Addr._____

18.   1 Peter 2:21,22
To this you were called,
because Christ suffered for you,
leaving you an example,   that
you should follow in **his** steps.
He committed no sin,   and
no deceit
was found in **his** mouth.
1 Pet. 2:21,22

18.   1 Peter 2:21,22
T t y w c,
b C s f y,
l y a e,   t
y s f i **h** s.
H c n s,   a
n d
w f i **h** m.
Addr._____

DAY 5: GLORIFYING GOD

19.   2 Corinthians 5:20
We are therefore
Christ's ambassadors,
as though God
were making **his** appeal
through us.
We implore you
on Christ's behalf:
Be reconciled to God.
2 Cor. 5:20

19.   2 Corinthians 5:20
W a t
C's a,
a t G
w m **h** a
t u.
W i y
o C's b:
B r t G.
Addr._____

20.   2 Corinthians 5:18
All this is from God,
who reconciled us
to **himself**
through Christ   and
gave us
the ministry of reconciliation:
2 Cor. 5:18

20.   2 Corinthians 5:18
A t i f G,
w r u
t **h**
t C   a
g u
t m o r:
Addr._____

21.   Romans 12:14,16,17,19
Bless those who persecute you;
bless   and
do not curse.
Live in harmony with one another.
Do not be proud,   but
be willing to associate
with people
of low position.
Do not be conceited.
Do not repay anyone
evil for evil.
Be careful to do
what is right ...
Do not take revenge, **my** friends,   but
leave room for God's wrath,
for it is written:
It is **mine** to avenge;
I will repay, says the Lord.
Rom. 12:14,16,17,19

21.   Romans 12:14,16,17,19
B t w p y;
b   a
d n c.
L i h w o a.
D n b p,   b
b w t a
w p
o l p.
D n b c.
D n r a
e f e.
B c t d
w i r ...
D n t r, **m** f,   b
l r f G's w,
f i i w:
I i **m** t a;
I w r, s t L.
Addr._____

22.   Romans 12:20a
On the contrary: [says the Lord]
If your enemy is hungry,
feed him;
if he is thirsty,
give him something to drink.
Rom. 12:20a

23.   Matthew 7:14
But small is the gate   and
narrow the road   that
leads to life,   and
only a few find it.
Mt. 7:14

24.   Genesis 1:21
So God created
the great creatures
of the sea   and
every living   and
moving thing
with which
the water teems,
according to their kinds,   and
every winged bird
according to its kind.   **And
God saw that it was good.**
Gen. 1:21

25.   Genesis 1:22,23
God blessed them   and said,
Be fruitful   and
increase in number   and
fill the water in the seas, and
let the birds increase
on the earth.   And
there was evening,   and
there was morning –
the fifth day.
Gen. 1:22,23

22.   Romans 12:20a
O t c:
I y e i h,
f h;
i h i t,
g h s t d.
Addr.____

23.   Matthew 7:14
B s i t g   a
n t r   t
l t l,   a
o a f f i.
Addr.____

24.   Genesis 1:21
S G c
t g c
o t s   a
e l   a
m t
w w
t w t,
a t t k,   a
e w b
a t i k. **A
G s t i w g.**
Addr.____

25.   Genesis 1:22,23
G b t   a s,
B f   a
i i n   a
f t w i t s,   a
l t b i
o t e.   A
t w e,   a
t w m –
t f d.
Addr.____

DAY SIX: ANALOGY SYNOPSIS

On Creation Day Six,
God's work in Creation was to create land animals –
livestock for domesticated animals, wild animals,
and "creeping thing"(KJV). In His image, God created
man – male and female. God presents to Adam, Eve,
his bride.

This reminds me of Christ creating His bride – the church
of sheep from every nation; but beforehand as the Lord
forewarned, deceiving wolves and "that old serpent"
will stir up self-worship among the sheep. Faithful sheep,
living out the two greatest commandments – of trusting
unreservedly in the Lord, and secondly, sharing His
reconciling love – will be ready when the Bridegroom
comes – Rev. 3:7-13. Jesus Christ will present to Himself
His bride.

ANALOGY: CREATION DAY SIX

Analogy: a partial likeness between two things that are compared. This analogy seeks to view the Scriptures about Jesus and the church through the narrative of Genesis Chapter One.

Creation Day 6: Genesis 1:24-31

24 And God said, "Let the land produce living creatures according to their kinds: livestock, creatures that move along the ground, and wild animals, each according to its kind." And it was so. 25 God made the wild animals according to their kinds, the livestock according to their kinds, and all the creatures that move along the ground according to their kinds. And God saw that it was good. 26 Then God said, "Let us make man in our image, in our likeness, and let them rule over the fish of the sea and the birds of the air, over the livestock, over all the earth, and over all the creatures that move along the ground." 27 So God created man in his own image, in the image of God he created him; male and female he created them. 28 God blessed them and said to them, "Be fruitful and increase in number; fill the earth and subdue it. Rule over the fish of the sea and the birds of the air and over every living creature that moves on the ground." 29 Then God said, "I give you every seed-bearing plant on the face of the whole earth and every tree that has fruit with seed in it. They will be yours for food. 30 And to all the beasts of the earth and all the birds of the air and all the creatures that move on the ground – everything that has the breath of life in it – I give every green plant for food." And it was so. 31 God saw all that he had made, and it was very good. And there was evening, and there was morning – the sixth day.

God's Work in Creation: God created land animals: domesticated and wild animals, and creeping things. In His own image, God created man – male and female.

Jesus' Work on Earth: Marriage: The church is awaiting her Bridegroom. Jesus forewarned about false prophets and false teachers deceiving many in the last days.

Bible Verse Keywords: Livestock; creatures that move along the ground; wild animals; sheep among wolves; false prophets ... in sheep's clothing; ferocious wolves; overflow of his heart; your words; mercy triumphs over judgement; why do you call me, Lord; on your guard against the yeast of the Pharisees; the good shepherd; lays down his life for the sheep; God created man in his own image; male and female; two shall become one flesh; concerning the church; cares; as Christ does the church; belong to another to him; Christ loved the church; gave himself up for her; a king ... prepared a wedding.

Pondered: 1. Land animals such as sheep, wolves, and serpent are created. Jesus said that in the last days, Satan, "that serpent of old," will deceive many, and so will wolves masquerading as sheep. Ever since the beautiful and anointed angel, Lucifer, later called Satan, measured and compared his self as best, one's eternity concludes on Christ's Lordship or fatal self-worship. True Christ-followers reject the satanic spirit of exalting self which poisoned a third of the holy angels, all earth, and for a time the Early Church.

2. Adam and Eve, Christ and His bride – each one flesh.

3. Could it be that some land animals bring to mind how Satan and false teachers deceive, while Adam and Eve are a typology of the Lord Jesus Christ marrying His bride – the church of sheep from every nation?

1.   Genesis 1:24
And God said,   Let the land produce
living creatures according to their kinds:
livestock,
creatures   that move
along the ground,   and
wild animals,
each according to its kind.   And
it was so.
Gen. 1:24

1.   Genesis 1:24
A G s,   L t l p
l c a t t k:
l,
c   t m
a t g,   a
w a,
e a t i k. A
i w s.
Addr._____

2.   Matthew 10:16; 7:15,16a
I am sending you out
like sheep among wolves.
Therefore be as shrewd
as snakes   and
as innocent as doves.
Watch out for false prophets.
They come to you   in sheep's clothing,   but
inwardly they are   ferocious wolves.
By their fruit   you will recognize them.
Mt. 10:16; 7:15,16a

2.   Matthew 10:16; 7:15,16a
I a s y o
l s a w.
T b a s
a s   a
a i a d.
W o f f p.
T c t y i s's c, b
i t a   f w.
B t f   y w r t.
Addr._____

3.   Luke 6:44a,45b; Matthew 12:36,37
Each tree is recognized
by its own fruit.
For out of the overflow
of his heart
his mouth speaks. Matthew 12:36,37

3.   Luke 6:44a,45b; Matthew 12:36,37
E t i r
b i o f.
F o o t o
o h h
h m s.

But I tell you   that
men will have to give account
on the day of judgment
for every careless word
they have spoken.
For by your words
you will be acquitted,   and
by your words
you will be condemned.
Lk. 6:44a,45b; Mt. 12:36,37

B I t y   t
m w h t g a
o t d o j
f e c w
t h s.
F b y w
y w b a, a
b y w
y w b c.
Addr._____

4.   Hebrews 13:15,16
Through Jesus, therefore,
let us continually offer to God
a sacrifice of praise –
the fruit of lips   that
confess **his** name.   And
do not forget to do good   and
to share with others,
for with such sacrifices
God is pleased.
Heb. 13:15,16

4.   Hebrews 13:15,16
T J, t,
l u c o t G
a s o p –
t f o l   t
c **h** n.   A
d n f t d g   a
t s w o,
f w s s
G i p.
Addr.____

5.   Matthew 25:31,33-37a,40
When the Son of Man
comes in **his** glory ...
he will sit on **his** throne
in heavenly glory.
He will put the sheep on **his** right   and
the goats on **his** left.
Then the King will say
to those on **his** right,
Come, you who are blessed by **my** Father;
take your inheritance,
the kingdom prepared for you
since the creation of the world.
For I was hungry   and you gave **me** something to eat,
I was thirsty   and you gave **me** something to drink,
I was a stranger   and you invited **me** in,
I needed clothes   and you clothed **me**,
I was sick   and you looked after **me**,
I was in prison   and you came to visit **me**.
Then the righteous will answer **him**,
Lord, when did we see you ...
The King will reply,
I tell you the truth,
whatever you did for one
of the least of these ...
you did for **me**.
Mt. 25:31,33-37a,40

5.   Matthew 25:31,33-37a,40
W t S o M
c i **h** g ...
h w s o **h** t
i **h** g.
H w p t s o **h** r   a
t g o **h** l.
T t K w s
t t o **h** r,
C, y w a b b **m** F;
t y i,
t k p f y
s t c o t w.
F I w h   a y g **m** s t e,
I w t   a y g **m** s t d,
I w a s   a y i **m** i,
I n c   a y c **m**,
I w s   a y l a **m**,
I w i p   a y c t v **m**.
T t r w a **h**,
L, w d w s y ...
T K w r,
I t y t t,
w y d f o
o t l o t ...
y d f **m**.
Addr.____

6.   James 2:13, Luke 6:36,46
because judgment without mercy
will be shown to anyone
who has not been merciful.
Mercy triumphs over judgment!
Be merciful,
just as your Father is merciful.
Why do you call **me**, Lord, Lord,   and
do not do what I say?
Js. 2:13, Lk. 6:36,46

6.   James 2:13, Luke 6:36,46
b j w m
w b s t a
w h n b m.
M t o j!
B m,
j a y F i m.
W d y c **m**, L, L,   a
d n d w I s?
Addr._____

7.   Luke 12:1b-3
Jesus began to speak first
to **his** disciples, saying:
Be on your guard against
the yeast of the Pharisees,
which is hypocrisy.
There is nothing concealed   that
will not be disclosed,   or
hidden that will not be made known.
What you have said in the dark
will be heard in the daylight,   and
what you have whispered in the ear
in the inner rooms
will be proclaimed from the roofs.
Lk. 12:1b-3

7.   Luke 12:1b-3
J b t s f
t **h** d, s:
B o y g a
t y o t P,
w i h.
T i n c   t
w n b d,   o
h t w n b m k.
W y h s i t d
w b h i t d, a
w y h w i t e
i t i r
w b p f t r.
Addr._____

8.   Matthew 7:12,13
So in everything,
do to others what
you would have them
do to you,
for this sums up
the Law   and the Prophets.
Enter through the narrow gate.
For wide is the gate   and
broad is the road   that
leads to destruction,   and
many enter through it.
Mt. 7:12,13

8.   Matthew 7:12,13
S i e,
d t o w
y w h t
d t y,
f t s u
t L   a t P.
E t t n g.
F w i t g   a
b i t r   t
l t d,   a
m e t i.
Addr._____

9.   John 10:7b,11,14b,15b
Jesus said again,
I tell you the truth,
I am the gate for the sheep.
I am the good shepherd.
The good shepherd
lays down **his** life   for the sheep.
I know **my** sheep   and
my sheep know **me** –   and
I lay down **my** life   for the sheep.
Jn. 10:7b,11,14b,15b

9.   John 10:7b,11,14b,15b
J s a,
I t y t t,
I a t g f t s.
I a t g s.
T g s
l d **h** l   f t s.
I k **m** s   a
m s k **m** –   a
I l d **m** l   f t s.
Addr.____

10.   Matthew 7:14
But small is the gate   and
narrow the road   that
leads to life,   and
only a few
find it.
Mt. 7:14

10.   Matthew 7:14
B s i t g   a
n t r   t
l t l,   a
o a f
f i.
Addr.____

11.   Genesis 1:25
God made the wild animals
according to their kinds,
the livestock according to their kinds,   and
all the creatures that move along the ground
according to their kinds.   **And**
God saw that it was good.
Gen. 1:25

11.   Genesis 1:25
G m t w a
a t t k,
t l a t t k,   a
a t c t m a t g
a t t k.   **A**
G s t i w g.
Addr.____

12.   Genesis 1:26
Then God said,
Let **us** make man
in **our** image,
in **our** likeness,   and
let them rule over the fish of the sea   and
the birds of the air,
over the livestock, over all the earth,   and
over all the creatures   that
move along the ground.
Gen. 1:26

12.   Genesis 1:26
T G s,
L **u** m m
i o i,
i o l,   a
l t r o t f o t s   a
t b o t a,
o t l, o a t e,   a
o a t c   t
m a t g.
Addr.____

13.   Genesis 1:27; 2:24
So God created man   in **his** own image,
in the image of God   **he** created him;
male and female   **he** created them. Genesis 2:24
That is why a man leaves
his father and mother   and
is united to his wife,   and
they become one flesh.
Gen. 1:27; 2:24

13.   Genesis 1:27; 2:24
S G c m   i **h** o i,
i t i o G   **h** c h;
m a f   **h** c t.
T i w a m l
h f a m   a
i u t h w,   a
t b o f.
Addr.____

14.   Ephesians 5:31,32
For this reason a man will leave
his father and mother   and
be united to his wife,   and
the two will become one flesh.
This is a profound mystery –   but
I am talking about Christ   and
the church.
Eph. 5:31,32

14.   Ephesians 5:31,32
F t r a m w l
h f a m   a
b u t h w,   a
t t w b o f.
T i a p m –   b
I a t a C   a
t c.
Addr.____

15.   Ephesians 5:29,30
After all, no one ever hated
his own body,   but
he feeds   and
cares for it,
just as Christ does the church –
for we are members
of **his** body.
Eph. 5:29,30

15.   Ephesians 5:29,30
A a, n o e h
h o b,   b
h f   a
c f i,
j a C d t c –
f w a m
o **h** b.
Addr.____

16.   Romans 7:4
So, my brothers,
you also died to the law
through the body of Christ,   that
you might belong to another,
to **him**
who was raised from the dead,
in order   that
we might bear fruit to God.
Rom. 7:4

16.   Romans 7:4
S, m b,
y a d t t l
t t b o C, t
y m b t a,
t **h**
w w r f t d,
i o   t
w m b f t G.
Addr.____

17. Ephesians 5:25b-27	17. Ephesians 5:25b-27
Christ loved the church and	C l t c a
gave **himself** up for her	g **h** u f h
to make her holy, cleansing her	t m h h, c h
by the washing with water	b t w w w
through the word, and	t t w, a
to present her to **himself**	t p h t **h**
as a radiant church, without stain or	a a r c, w s o
wrinkle or any other blemish, but	w o a o b, b
holy and blameless.	h a b.
Eph. 5:25b-27	Addr.____

18. Matthew 22:2,8,10-12a	18. Matthew 22:2,8,10-12a
The kingdom of heaven is like a king	T k o h i l a k
who prepared a wedding banquet for his son.	w p a w b f h s.
Then he said to his servants,	T h s t h s,
The wedding banquet is ready, but	T w b i r, b
those I invited did not deserve to come.	t I i d n d t c.
So the servants went out into the streets and	S t s w o i t s a
gathered all the people they could find,	g a t p t c f,
both good and bad, and	b g a b, a
the wedding hall was filled with guests. But	t w h w f w g. B
when the king came in to see the guests,	w t k c i t s t g,
he noticed a man there	h n a m t
who was not wearing wedding clothes.	w w n w w c.
Friend, he asked, how did you get in here	F, h a, h d y g i h
without wedding clothes?	w w c?
Mt. 22:2,8,10-12a	Addr.____

19. 1 Corinthians 1:29,30	19. 1 Corinthians 1:29,30
so that no one may boast	s t n o m b
before **him**.	b **h**.
It is because of **him** that	I i b o **h** t
you are in Christ Jesus,	y a i C J,
who has become for us	**w** h b f u
wisdom from God – that is,	w f G – t i,
our righteousness,	o r,
holiness and	h a
redemption.	r.
1 Cor. 1:29,30	Addr.____

20.   Matthew 25:1,5-10
At that time the kingdom of heaven will be like
ten virgins who took their lamps   and
went out to meet the bridegroom.
The bridegroom was a long time in coming,   and
they all became drowsy and fell asleep.
At midnight the cry rang out:
Here's the bridegroom!   Come out to meet him!
Then all the virgins woke up   and
trimmed their lamps. [The wise had oil with them.]
The foolish ones said to the wise,
Give us some of your oil ...
No, they replied, there may not be enough ...
Instead, go to those who sell oil and buy ...   But
while they [the foolish] were on their way to buy ...
the bridegroom arrived.
The virgins who were ready
went in with him to the wedding banquet.   And
the door was shut.
Mt. 25:1,5-10

20.   Matthew 25:1,5-10
A t t t k o h w b l
t v w t t l   a
w o t m t b.
T b w a l t i c,   a
t a b d a f a.
A m t c r o:
H's t b!   C o t m h!
T a t v w u   a
t t l.
T f o s t t w,
G u s o y o ...
N, t r, t m n b e ...
I, g t t w s o a b ... B
w t w o t w t b ...
t b a.
T v w w r
w i w h t t w b.   A
t d w s.
Addr.____

21.   Luke 10:25,26a,29-34a,36a,37
... an expert in the law stood ... to test Jesus. Teacher,
he asked, what must I do to inherit eternal life?
[Jesus said] What is written in the Law? ...   But
[the lawyer] he wanted to justify himself, [quoted the
two greatest commandments and] so he asked Jesus,
And who is my neighbor?
In reply Jesus said ... A priest ... passed by ...
So too,   a Levite ... passed by
on the other side [of a half dead man].   But
a Samaritan ... came where the man was;   and
when he saw him,   he took pity on him.
He went to him   and ... took care of him ...
Which of these three
do you think was a neighbor to the man ...
The expert in the law replied,
The one who had mercy on him.
Jesus told him [the lawyer], Go and do likewise.
Lk. 10:25,26a,29-34a,36a,37

21.   Luke 10:25,26a,29-34a,36a,37
... a e i t l s ... t t J. T,
h a, w m I d t i e l?
W i w i t L? ...   B
h w t j h,
s h a J,
A w i m n?
I r J s ... A p ... p b ...
S t,   a L ... p b
o t o s.   B
a S ... c w t m w;   a
w h s h, h t p o h.
H w t h a ... t c o h ...
W o t t
d y t w a n t t m ...
T e i t l r,
T o w h m o h.
J t h, G a d l.
Addr.____

22. Galatians 3:1,3
You foolish Galatians!
Who has bewitched you?
Before your very eyes
Jesus Christ was clearly portrayed
as crucified.
Are you so foolish?
After beginning
with the Spirit,
are you now trying to attain
your goal by human effort?
Gal. 3:1,3

22. Galatians 3:1,3
Y f G!
W h b y ?
B y v e
J C w c p
a c.
A y s f ?
A b
w t S,
a y n t t a
y g b h e ?
Addr.____

23. 1 Corinthians 15:50,51
I declare to you, brothers,   that
flesh and blood
cannot inherit the kingdom of God,   nor
does the perishable
inherit the imperishable.
Listen, I tell you a mystery:
We will not all sleep,   but
we will all be changed –
1 Cor. 15:50,51

23. 1 Corinthians 15:50,51
I d t y, b,   t
f a b
c i t k o G, n
d t p
i t i.
L, I t y a m:
W w n a s, b
w w a b c –
Addr.____

24. Matthew 25:13
Therefore keep watch,
because you do not know
the day or the hour [Jesus will come].
Mt. 25:13

24. Matthew 25:13
T k w,
b y d n k
t d o t h.
Addr.____

25. Genesis 1:28
God blessed them   and said to them,
Be fruitful   and
increase in number;
fill the earth   and subdue it.
Rule over the fish of the sea   and
the birds of the air   and
over every living creature   that
moves on the ground.
Gen. 1:28

25. Genesis 1:28
G b t   a s t t,
B f   a
i i n;
f t e   a s i.
R o t f o t s a
t b o t a   a
o e l c   t
m o t g.
Addr.____

26. Genesis 1:29,30	26. Genesis 1:29,30
Then God said, I give you	T G s, I g y
every seed-bearing plant	e s-b p
on the face of the whole earth and	o t f o t w e a
every tree that has fruit with seed in it.	e t t h f w s i i.
They will be yours for food. And	T w b y f f. A
to all the beasts of the earth and	t a t b o t e a
all the birds of the air and	a t b o t a a
all the creatures that	a t c t
move on the ground –	m o t g –
everything that	e t
has the breath of life in it –	h t b o l i i –
I give every green plant for food. And	I g e g p f f. A
it was so.	i w s.
Gen. 1:29,30	Addr._____
27. John 6:51	27. John 6:51
[Jesus said] I am the living bread ...	I a t l b ...
This bread is **my** flesh,	T b i **m** f,
which I ... give	w I ... g
for the life of the world.	f t l o t w.
Jn. 6:51	Addr._____
28. John 12:26	28. John 12:26
Whoever serves **me**	W s **m**
must follow **me**; and	m f **m**; a
where I am,	w I a,
my servant also will be.	**m** s a w b.
My Father will honor the one	M F w h t o
who serves **me**.	w s **m**.
Jn. 12:26	Addr._____
29. Genesis 1:31	29. Genesis 1:31
God saw all **that**	**G s a** **t**
he had made, **and**	**h h m,** **a**
it was very good. And	**i w v g.** A
there was evening, and	t w e, a
there was morning –	t w m –
the sixth day.	t s d.
Gen. 1:31	Addr._____

DAY SEVEN: ANALOGY SYNOPSIS

On Day Seven,
God rested from His work. Creation is finished.
God blessed the seventh day and sanctified it.

This reminds me that Jesus rested from His work;
the sacrifice is finished. He blessed the whole world
for He secured "the way" of direct access to Holy
God, and the sanctification of His disciples.

Jesus Christ glorified His Father on earth, and in
heaven Father God glorified His Son – the victorious
Lamb – the true Light.

ANALOGY: GOD RESTED

God's Work of Creation Is Finished. Jesus' Work, to Die to Save Sinners, Is Finished; He Lives.

Day 7: Genesis 2:1-3

1 Thus the heavens and the earth were completed in all their vast array. 2 By the seventh day God had finished the work he had been doing; so on the seventh day he rested from all his work. 3 And God blessed the seventh day and made it holy, because on it he rested from all the work of creating that he had done.

God's Work in Creation: Done: God is finished. He rested on the seventh day.

Jesus' Work on Earth: Done: Jesus Christ is finished; He died on the cross for our sins and paid our penalty of death – once for all. Before His crucifixion, Jesus secured from His Father, the perfect Counselor and Helper for His disciples – the Holy Spirit. Thereby once resurrected, the Lord Jesus Christ sat down at His Father's right hand – at rest from His atoning work on earth.

Bible Verse Keywords: Thus the heavens and the earth ... were completed; the seventh day God finished the work; he rested; It is finished; rose early on the first day of the week; he ... was taken up to heaven; he sat at the right hand of God;

Pondered: 1. The heavens and the earth were finished, and God rested from all His work. He blessed the seventh day and sanctified it. The sentence of death for every man, woman, and child was paid; "It is finished." Jesus is at rest from all His sacrificial, substitutionary work.

2. Hebrews10:14b says, "By one sacrifice he has made perfect forever those who are being made holy." Eph. 5:25b,26 declares, "Just as Christ loved the church and gave himself up for her to make her holy, cleansing her by the washing with water through the word." Jesus, Who knew no sin, bore our sins, so we might become His righteousness before His Holy Father.

3. Jesus said to His Father in John17:4,5, **"I have brought you glory on earth by completing the work you gave me to do. And now, Father, glorify me in your presence with the glory I had with you before the world began."**

4. Thus the resurrected Jesus Christ was carried up to heaven and received by His Father. Christ sat down at His Father's right hand.

5. With the return of His Son – the victorious Mediator, God sent the Holy Spirit – the Counselor Helper. Now He is at work on earth drawing people to Jesus, indwelling believers, sanctifying and filling them, speaking and teaching of Christ, and empowering disciples to be like their Savior Lord.

6. The Lord Jesus Christ is at work in heaven preparing a place for each disciple transformed by His finished cross work and His Lordship.

DAY 7: LIVING HOPE

MEDITATION SCRIPTURES

1.   Genesis 2:1-3
Thus the heavens and the earth
were completed
in all their vast array.
By the seventh day
God had finished the work
he had been doing;
so on the seventh day
he rested
from all **his** work.

And God blessed the seventh day   and
made it holy,
because on it
he rested from all the work
of creating   that
he had done.
Gen. 2:1-3

1.   Genesis 2:1-3
T t h a t e
w c
i a t v a.
B t s d
G h f t w
h h b d;
s o t s d
h r
f a **h** w.

A G b t s d   a
m i h,
b o i
h r f a t w
o c   t
h h d.
Addr._____

2.   John 19:28a,30b; Luke 23:46b
Later, knowing that all
was now completed,   and
so that the Scripture
would be fulfilled ...
Jesus said, ... It is finished.   Luke 23:46b
When **he** had said this,
he breathed **his** last.
Jn. 19:28a,30b; Lk. 23:46b

2.   John 19:28a,30b; Luke 23:46b
L, k t a
w n c,   a
s t t S
w b f ...
J s, ... I i f.
W **h** h s t,
h b **h** l.
Addr._____

3.   Mark 16:9a,14a,19b; Luke 24:50b,51
... Jesus rose early
on the first day of the week,
Later Jesus appeared to the Eleven ... Lk. 24:51
he lifted up **his** hands   and blessed them.
While **he** was blessing them,
he left them   and Mark 16:19b
was taken up into heaven.   and
he sat at the right hand of God.
Mk. 16:9a,14a,19b; Lk. 24:50b,51

3.   Mark16:9a,14a,19b; Luke 24:50b,51
... J r e
o t f d o t w,
L J a t t E ...
h l u **h** h   a b t.
W **h** w b t,
h l t   a
w t u i h.   a
h s a t r h o G.
Addr._____

4.   Colossians 1:19,20
For God was pleased
to have all **his** fullness dwell
in **him**,   and through **him**
to reconcile to **himself** all things,
whether things on earth   or
things in heaven,
by making peace
through **his** blood,
shed on the cross.
Col. 1:19,20

4.   Colossians 1:19,20
F G w p
t h a **h** f d
i **h**,   a t **h**
t r t **h** a t,
w t o e o
t i h,
b m p
t **h** b,
s o t c.
Addr._____

5.   1 Timothy 2:5,6a
For there is one God   and
one **mediator** between God   and men,
the **man** Christ Jesus,
who gave **himself**
as a ransom for all men –
1 Tim. 2:5,6a

5.   1 Timothy 2:5,6a
F t i o G   a
o **m** b G   a m,
t **m** C J,
w g **h**
a a r f a m –
Addr._____

6.   1 Peter 1:3,4
Praise be to the God   and
Father of our Lord Jesus Christ!
In **his** great mercy
he has given us new birth
into a living hope
through the resurrection of Jesus Christ
from the dead,   and
into an inheritance   that
can never perish, spoil   or fade –
kept in heaven for you,
1 Pet. 1:3,4

6.   1 Peter 1:3,4
P b t t G a
F o o L J C!
I **h** g m
h h g u n b
i a l h
t t r o J C
f t d,   a
i a i   t
c n p, s o f –
k i h f y,
Addr._____

7.   1 John 4:9
This is how God showed
his love among us:
He sent **his** one   and only Son
into the world   that
we might live through **him**.
1 Jn. 4:9

7.   1 John 4:9
T i h G s
h l a u:
H s **h** o a o S
i t w   t
w m l t **h**.
Addr._____

8.   Romans 15:13
May the God of hope
fill you with all joy   and
peace as you trust
in **him**,   so that
you may overflow with hope
by the power of the Holy Spirit.
Rom. 15:13

8.   Romans 15:13
M t G o h
f y w a j   a
p a y t
i **h**,   s t
y m o w h
b t p o t H S.
Addr._____

9.   Romans 1:20a
For since the creation of the world
God's invisible qualities –
his eternal power   and
divine nature –
have been clearly seen,
being understood from
what has been made,
Rom. 1:20a

9.   Romans 1:20a
F s t c o t w
G's i q –
h e p a
d n –
h b c s,
b u f
w h b m,
Addr._____

10.   John 1:9
The true **light**   that
gives light to every man
was coming into the world.
Jn. 1:9

10.   John 1:9
T t **l** t
g l t e m
w c i t w.
Addr._____

11.   Revelation 21:2
I [Apostle John] saw the Holy City,
the new Jerusalem,
coming down out of heaven from God,
prepared as a bride beautifully dressed
for her **husband**.
Rev. 21:2

11.   Revelation 21:2
I s t H C,
t n J,
c d o o h f G,
p a a b b d
f h **h**.
Addr._____

12.   Revelation 21:23
The city does not need the sun   or
the moon to shine on it,
for the glory of God
gives it light,   and (KJV)
the Lamb is the light ...
Rev. 21:23

12.   Revelation 21:23
T c d n n t s o
t m t s o i,
f t g o G
g i l,   a
t L i t l ...
Addr._____

EPILOGUE: THE ESSENTIALS

HOW TO BE SAVED / RECEIVE CHRIST IN YOUR HEART

Holy God Creator,

I, _____, on _____ __, 2____.
    (name)   (date)

Admit that I am a sinner, and I deserve Your penalty of death for sin. I am sorry for my sins, and sincerely ask you to forgive me.

I:

Believe that Jesus Christ is Your Son and God. He paid my penalty of death when He died on the cross for my sins. He rose on the third day; therefore, I am assured that the penalty for my sin was paid and accepted. My forgiveness is only through faith in Jesus' sacrifice for me.

I:

Confess that I have received Your gift of forgiveness, and desire You to control my life. Now I am *a child of God.* I am an imitator of Jesus Christ empowered by God to turn away from sin and live victoriously for Christ. I am *a believer, saved, an heir of God with eternal life.*
Now Jesus Christ is my Lord, Master, and Savior.

LORDSHIP: TWO GREATEST COMMANDMENTS

The most important one,

answered Jesus,

is this ...

Love the Lord your God

with all your heart and

with all your soul and

with all your mind and

with all your strength.

The second is this:

Love your neighbor

as yourself.

There is no commandment

greater than these.
Mark 12:29-31

THE HOLY BIBLE: THE LIVING WORD OF GOD

For the word of God is living and active. Sharper than any double-edged sword, it penetrates even to dividing soul and spirit, joints and marrow; it judges the thoughts and attitudes of the heart. Nothing in all creation is hidden from God's sight. Everything is uncovered and laid bare before the eyes of him to whom we must give account. Hebrews 4:12,13

If in reading this book, you prayed and received Jesus Christ into your heart as your Savior and Lord, please tell us.